DRIFT

"In a *dérive*, one or more persons during a certain period drop their relations, their work
and leisure activities, and all their other usual motives for movement and action, and let
themselves be drawn by the attractions of the terrain and the encounters they find there."
— Guy Debord, *Theory of the Dérive*, 1958.

The translation of *dérive* is *drift*.

BALI

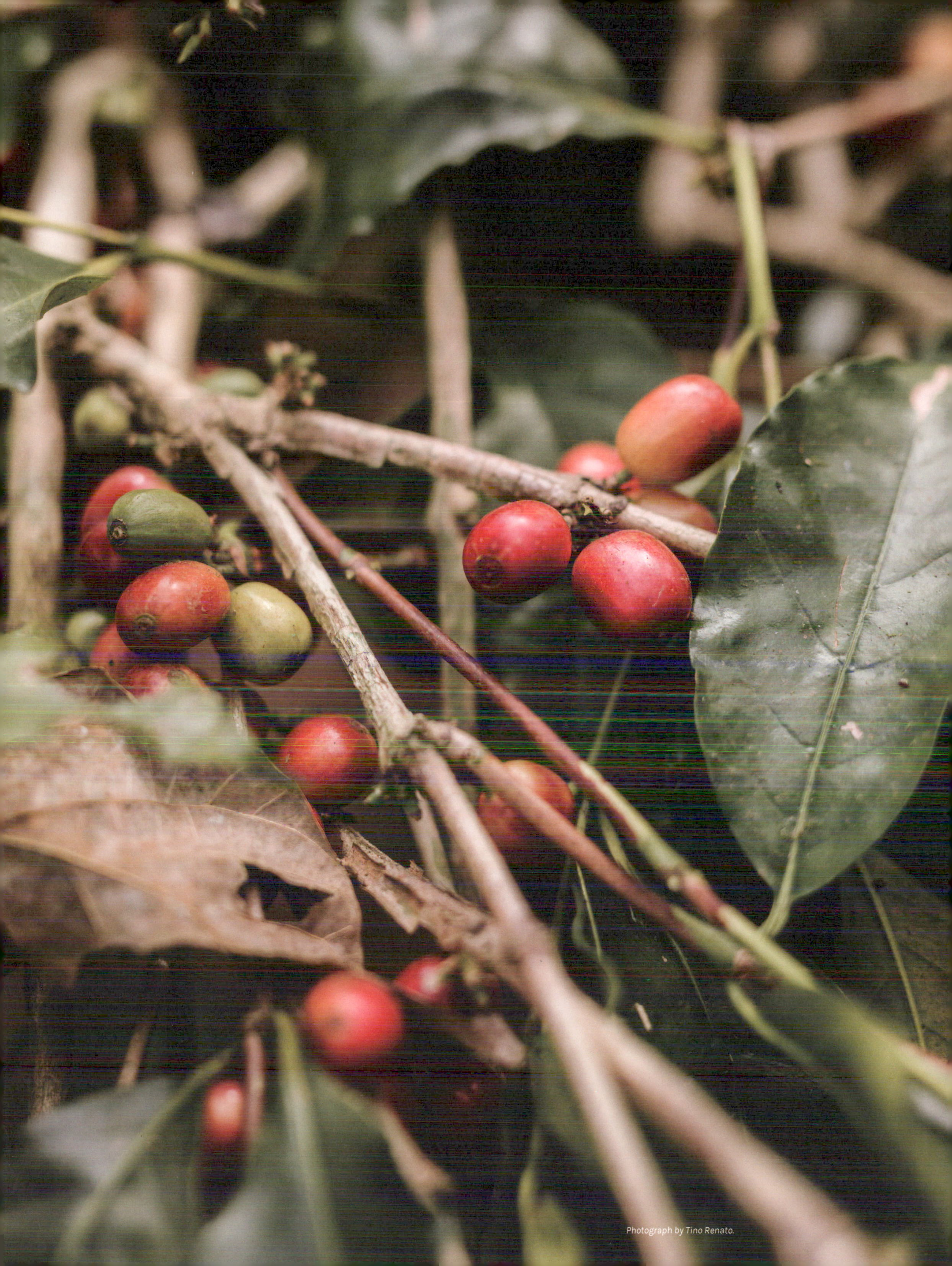

Photograph by Tino Renato.

ADAM GOLDBERG
Editor in Chief

DANIELA VELASCO
Creative Director

ELYSSA GOLDBERG
Editorial Director

BONJWING LEE
Executive Editor

CONTRIBUTORS
Anita Surewicz
Austin Langlois
Dale Arden Chong
David Buehrer
Ecky Prabanto
Imogen Lepere
Jacqueline Larkin
Kayleigh Rattle
Keng Pereira
Lauren Rebbeck
Michelle Anindya
Nicholas O'Hara-Boyd
Ole Tillmann
Sabrina Sucato
Santiago Rodriguez Tarditi
Thomas Wensma
Tino Renato

TO OUR READERS

For our ninth edition of *Drift*, we travel to Bali, a lush and tropical island in Southeast Asia. Located in predominantly Muslim Indonesia, where alcohol is culturally discouraged in religious regions, Bali has become an important source of coffee in an archipelago nation, where 300 million kilograms of it are consumed each year.

Although it is part of Indonesia, Bali, at times, feels like another world. The island is culturally Hindu with its own unique collection of rituals not celebrated elsewhere in Indonesia. Offerings to the gods—what the Balinese call *canang sari*—of small palm-leaf baskets filled with wild flowers, fruit, rice, incense, and coffee adorn the winding streets each morning, inviting good spirits and keeping the bad ones at bay. Within the island itself, the regions differ significantly from each other, both culturally and geographically. From the all-night beachside parties amongst the gridlock of mopeds in Seminyak to the quiet, endless rice paddies and mountainside yoga studios in Ubud, Bali can feel like many countries in one to the many foreigners who visit each year. Added to this are the island's ever-increasing influences from abroad, brought by Australian and European tourists. Yet food and coffee unite this seemingly disparate island culture.

For most, coffee is not the first thought that comes to mind when thinking of Bali. Perhaps it should be. After the popularity of the film *Eat Pray Love*, Bali is often imagined as a soul-searching retreat for self-discovery or a weekend party escape from neighboring Australia. But in this striking patchwork of cultures saturated with tourism, a specialty coffee scene is exploding.

In the northern highlands of Kintamani, the rich volcanic soils and favorable climate produce a citrusy and full-bodied coffee with balanced acidity. Historically, Kintamani coffee has been exported globally, to countries as far away as the United States. However, domestic consumption is growing rapidly, driven by coffee-drinkers in Bali. Rodney Glick and Kadek Edi of Seniman Coffee consider this trend of consuming coffee in the place where it is grown as the "fourth wave," and have created a modified SCAA tasting wheel with domestic flavor references to enhance local coffee grading quality. As many of Bali's finest coffees do not leave the island, you will have to visit to taste them.

As the island's sultry jungles, cascading waterfalls, and warm and friendly people continue to gain popularity among foreigners, Bali's infrastructure struggles to keep apace, and the negative impact on the local ecosystem is becoming alarmingly apparent. While enterprising Australians have brought avocado toast, chia seed puddings, and flat whites to designer cafes that cater to tourists and locals alike, many of these shops have also began to focus on environmental sustainability to minimize the impact that tourism is having on the island.

Drift, Bali guides us from Canggu to Ubud to Kintamani and catalogues a variety of drinks, from *kopi* durian (coffee with durian) to *bajigur* (coffee with coconut milk and brown sugar), as we attempt to uncover the exciting things brewing in Bali's coffee scene.

Adam Goldberg,
Editor in Chief

17,000 Islands of Coffee Drinks

WORDS Michelle Anindya
PHOTOGRAPHS Tino Renato

I sit in front of a plate of durian and a cup of coffee. The durian is just slightly overripe, its tender meat begins to seep alcohol. You're supposed to drink them together, my friend told me. Even for an Indonesian, the thought of combining these two dominant flavors is repulsive. Yet, on the island of Sumatra, just a five-hour flight from Bali, *kopi durian* is a local favorite.

Even with the specialty coffee industry revealing another side of coffee and opening new conversations around brewing methods, in rural areas, you'll still find coffee treated as a spice. And, in an archipelago country comprised of thousands of islands, you can imagine the variety of ways that Indonesians use it. The West Sumatran men will mix brewed coffee with beaten eggs as a potent energy drink. The Manadonese will add ginger and crunchy *kenari* (local almonds) to their coffee. In Sumatra, those with durian trees might mix coffee with puréed durian pulp. And in the areas where it's hilly and chilly, a warm drink of brown sugar, coconut milk, and coffee called *bajigur*, has become a timeless favorite.

During and after the commodification of coffee by the Dutch, the good stuff was exported and everything else—fondly called *kopi jagung* or corn coffee—was left for local consumption. To make it less painful to consume, Indonesians add corn kernels, rice, or *kenari* while roasting the beans and a heaping teaspoon of sugar into the hot drink—a cheap, no-fuss method we've come to love. The dark bitter coffee becomes a blank canvas from which a concoction of flavors arises. And typically, these coffee drinks are highly sugared and flavored, just the way Indonesians like it.

Some would argue that these spices are just cosmetic flavorings to help cover up the bitterness of coffee, as well as the bitterness of colonialism. But whether we're mixing brewed coffee with palm sugar or coconut water, these are our creative, utilitarian survival mechanisms that are very Indonesian, in the best possible way.

Indonesia's colorful and eccentric approach to drinking coffee sits in stark contrast to the more refined, clean approach of specialty coffee. Like Indonesian meals, which are gloriously unstructured and flavorful—an explosion of tropical herbs and spices—so too are Indonesia's many coffee drinks.

Kopi gula aren (palm sugar)

Kopi regal, Warung Ipang Bali

Tubruk

TUBRUK

This drink is made in the simplest way possible—finely ground coffee topped with boiling water, then sugar to your liking (Indonesians love to make it extra sweet). But ask anyone who is usually responsible for making *tubruk* for the family and you'd find a multitude of ways to brew it. Some people will let it steep until all of the dregs sink to the bottom; others cover their cup with a lid for a few minutes before drinking; and the new baristas will meticulously measure the amount of water and the grind level to make a more refined *tubruk*. In fact, due to its simple brewing method, *tubruk* is exactly the way professional cuppers score beans. As an Indonesian farmer, who was invited to attend a cupping session in Germany, once scoffed, "We do cuppings every day—called *tubruk!*"

The robusta beans typically used in *tubruk* give it a proper caffeine punch. Popular in Indonesia, this deeply aromatic brew is the perfect breakfast coffee. Served with a plate of fried bananas or *dadar gulung* (soft pancake with banana slices, grated coconut, and a drizzle of honey), and for those who prefer, a pack of clove cigarettes, this drink—often spiked with sugar—is the perfect wake-up call.

KOPI DURIAN

The presence of durian can be abhorrent to some people. Just like its appallingly thorny appearance, durian attracts those with an appetite for peculiar culinary adventures. Drunk with black coffee, durian traditionally acts as a sweetener and creamer. The key is to choose a perfectly ripe durian for its maximum sweetness with a tad of alcohol for that slight layer of buzz. But remember to drink this wisely—combining durian with coffee certainly takes some guts and is not what you'd call an everyday coffee drink.

BAJIGUR

Originating from the highlands of West Java, *bajigur* is basically coconut milk and brown sugar, with the addition of coffee (usually robusta), ginger, and salt to taste. The resulting drink is sweet, salty, creamy, full-bodied—an exotic compilation of flavors. Anyone who visits the highlands of West Java can easily find themselves huddled underneath a *warung kopi*, seeking warmth and comfort from this soupy, coconut drink. A popular drink among Javanese, *bajigur* is the ultimate "hug in a cup," especially in the evening!

KOPI TAKAR

Another drink redolent of the tropics is *kopi takar*—brewed coffee served in a cup made out of coconut shell and drank with a cinnamon straw. The locals in the Mandailing region of Sumatra enjoy *kopi takar* with a slice of fudgey, creamy palm sugar that melts in the mouth as you drink the brew. *Kopi takar* is their version of an elegant, simple black coffee. It can be found in any local eatery in Sumatra for less than a dollar.

KOPI TALUA

Kopi talua literally means "egg-yolk coffee." Its unusual, *jamu*-like (herbal drink) scent adds to its mysterious alchemy-like promises of enhancing libido, as well as weight loss. Originating from Padang in West Sumatra, *kopi talua* is made by whisking egg yolk—usually from free-range chickens—with *lidi* (a strip of coconut palm frond stalk) or an electric hand mixer until it's thick, foamy, and creamy. Boiling-hot coffee—already sweetened—is poured over the whipped yolk, cooking the egg, resulting in what locals believe to be a potent energy drink. It's a drink that needs a lot of sweetener, whether that's coconut milk, sweetened condensed milk, palm sugar, or refined sugar, which can be added while brewing the coffee, or with the egg-yolk before being whisked together. And to mask the under-cooked aroma, lime, vanilla, or cinnamon is often dashed on top of the drink. There are many variations to this egg-yolk coffee. In South Sulawesi for example, egg-yolk coffee is made with an added mixture of ginger, palm sugar, and coconut milk. Regardless, the real seduction of *kopi talua* is in its curative claims.

Thus is the diversity of Indonesia's traditional coffee drinks, a dynamic family that contrasts starkly with the Indonesian specialty coffee scene. –

Kopi alpukat (avocado), Warung Ipang Bali

A Lesson In Simplicity and Waiting

WORDS Austin Langlois
PHOTOGRAPHS Adam Goldberg

I remember the first time I tasted Bali coffee (or Bali *kopi*, as locals know it).

I had just landed on the island after a 26-hour journey from Chicago. After the hour-plus drive to my villa hotel, nestled in a highland village lined with rice patties called Ubud, I was ready for a caffeine fix. After ordering a coffee, I padded down to soak my tired feet in my private pool.

Sitting there, the sweet breeze perfumed by the overhanging frangipani trees, I took my first sip of this nectar of the gods.

And, immediately I spit it out—my mouth full of coffee grounds.

Apparently, it's a common mistake that Bali newbies make. When you're offered coffee, unless you specify drip coffee or an espresso-based coffee (like an Americano or latte) you're usually offered Bali coffee. It's a local type of instant coffee, often made with both finely ground coffee and coffee powder, that's either boiled with water, or spooned into a mug of hot water and stirred together. Traditional shops that are popular with the locals, like Kedai Kopi Aboe Thalib in central Bali, still brew Bali coffee with a pan of boiling water on the stove.

In a way, it's reminiscent of Turkish or Greek coffee, as the result is a strongly brewed, boiled coffee. Just without the fancy coffee pot (*cezve* or *briki*).

As I would learn, you have to wait for the coffee grounds to settle to the bottom.

…

Although Indonesia has been well-known for its coffee, it has only been in the last century that its cultivation has moved to Bali. Other Indonesian islands, like Sumatra, produce most of the coffee crop, which is exported to other countries. This is usually arabica beans.

While Bali does have a blossoming organic arabica trade—and among coffee roasters, coffee regions like Kintamani (the northern part of the island) have growing acclaim—the traditional Bali coffee is made from robusta beans. As such, Bali coffee has an earthier, more bitter taste and is widely consumed by locals due to its affordable price. Robusta also has almost twice the amount of caffeine as arabica. While locals have adjusted to the higher caffeine content, it causes noticeable jitters among unacquainted visitors.

Asher Yaron, who founded F.R.E.A.K. Coffee, a boutique coffee roastery and cafe in Ubud, shared a similar initial reaction to Bali coffee as I had.

"On my first visit to Bali in 1997, I thought the coffee was so bad that I couldn't drink it," said Yaron. "For the duration of my stay in Bali I stopped drinking coffee completely and drank tea instead. When I permanently moved here in 2010, not much had changed regarding the quality of the coffee available."

In an effort to bring better coffee to the masses, he began buying arabica beans (which was uncommon for that time) from coffee farmers in Kintamani, and roasting himself. Today, craft coffee shops with artsy lattes dot the streets of Bali's larger cities, buying and roasting arabica beans, while locals continue to drink their Bali coffee made with robusta beans. In many ways, it's the tale of two islands—just a further example of difference between living in Bali and visiting.

While I love the morning ritual of grinding beans and brewing my pour over, there's a simplicity in Bali coffee. Waiting for the grounds to sink to the bottom is a reminder to slow down—a morning meditation that's part of the island life.

—

Cup of Happiness

WORDS Jacqueline Larkin
PHOTOGRAPHS Tino Renato

In 2014, the International Coffee Organization reported that Indonesia was the fourth largest producer of coffee in the world. Known for producing mainly robusta beans alongside some high-status, specialty arabica blends, Indonesia's coffee production is a long-standing, geographically dispersed agricultural tradition. Indonesia's diverse geographies, combined with the country's distinct cultures and localised processing systems, have resulted in a range of attributes that define the region's flagship blends. Approximately 95% of production originates from small landholders farming an average of one to two hectares of land. A notable portion of these modest plantations are nestled in the lush highlands of Bali—a region where agricultural practices are guided by a deep-rooted reverence for the natural environment inspired by Hindu philosophy. Bali's coffee producers have been able to tap into Fairtrade and organic markets, which similarly center on environmental sustainability, ecological conservation, and ethical farming, which the region's traditions have historically embraced.

Unlike other parts of Indonesia—such as Java and Sumatra—coffee grown in Bali wasn't established by the Dutch. The origins of Bali's coffee production can be traced to the beginning of the 20th century, when traders from Lombok—an Indonesian island east of Bali—brought coffee plants to the area. The Kintamani region of Bali, known for its rich volcanic soil and favourable micro-climates, was ideally-suited for growing coffee, and small-scale farms soon developed. The establishment of coffee as an agricultural stronghold was in part owed to the variety of coffee imported to Bali, known as robusta. The robusta strain is a hearty plant highly resistant to disease and insects. Unlike other varieties, robusta coffee thrives in lower altitudes and is able to withstand adverse climate conditions. The world's second most popular and widely consumed coffee—a close runner up to the arabica blend—the robusta bean produces a bold, bitter, and full-bodied brew, with a distinct earthy flavour.

By contrast, arabica is a notably more fickle strain of coffee, more susceptible to the natural elements and known for producing less predictable yields. The arabica coffee plant is grown in the highlands of the Kintamani region—a major coffee-growing district located in the northeastern part of Bali. Regarded as a high-quality coffee, arabica accounts for approximately 60 to 70 percent of the world's coffee consumption. It possesses a palatable flavour profile that is sweeter and subtler with a milder acidity. Certain blends possess fruity notes with flavours of berries, while others have hints of caramel and chocolate, such as the Cataui variety.

Most of Bali's coffee is produced by local farmers organized under a traditional agricultural system called Subak Abian. The Subak Abian system functions similar to a cooperative, whereby Balinese farmers pool resources and frequently collaborate on the financial, technical, social, and religious aspects related to agriculture. Operating under the guiding philosophy of Tri Hita Karana, Subaks subscribe to a Hindu belief system that emphasizes the importance of maintaining a harmonious relationship between oneself and God, other humans, and the natural environment. The teachings of Tri Hita Karana promote a deep reverence for nature by emphasizing humanity's communal dependence on the life-sustaining forces of the natural world—a doctrine that has undoubtedly fortified the region's long-standing commitment to environmental preservation. The environmentally inclined tenants of Tri Hita Karana blend well with the eco-friendly ethics of Fairtrade, particularly in regards to sustainability and conservation. Fairtrade certification often requires its producers to own a parcel of land for the breeding of animals or the multi-purpose cultivation of produce. Under the Subak Abian system, Balinese farmers typically generate additional income through mixed farming and crop diversification, such as the harvesting of trees for citrus fruits and timber. Cultivated tree-growth provides permanent shade to create a favourable microclimate for coffee bushes, while also preventing soil erosion during the rainy season. Tall elephant grass lining the fields provides a "green" source of feed for cattle. This natural food source produces organic manure to enrich soil used to fertilize coffee bushes, while also supporting local biodiversity, including insects and birds. This synergistic approach to agriculture aligns with the holistic benefits of organic farming, which emphasizes the use of biological fertilizers and naturally-derived pest controls over synthetic or chemically-based ones.

In 2008, Kintamani arabica became the first product in Indonesia to receive a Geographical Identification. Geographical Identifications, or GIs, protect consumer goods that meet certain territorial criteria with an official designation. By certifying the regional characteristics upon which a product's reputation is built, GIs provide a degree of legal protection by placing constraints on competitors attempting to market counterfeit goods. Examples of renowned products that are GI certified, include: Champagne produced from grapes grown in the Champagne region of France, Cuban cigars rolled from Cuban tobacco leaves, Parmesan cheese named after the producing region in Italy, and Swiss watches manufactured in Switzerland. Agricultural products often retain qualities from their place of origin that are influenced by local factors, such as climate and soil. GIs not only capture the value and authenticity of these place-related characteristics, but are often promoted as a development initiative for rural communities, with the intention of improving livelihoods and alleviating poverty. As a product's reputation spreads beyond borders and demand increases, a community of producers are able to channel investment toward the conservation of natural resources and traditional knowledge from which their products were derived.

In the coffee world, GI certification is a badge of origin that signifies quality and identity-based prestige amongst distributors. It guarantees to consumers that the coffee produced is from a specific geographic

Left: Pak Ketut Suar. Right: Sri Wenten & Putu Trisna Widyastuti.

region where precise methods of cultivation were applied. For example, the arabica coffee originating from Bali's Kintamani zone, known as Kopi Arabika Kintamani Bali, is a GI certified and internationally recognized blend valued for its high quality. In the Kintamani highlands, at an altitude above 900 metres, lies the volcanic Mount Batur. Here the fertile soil, favourable landforms, and temperate climate are ideal conditions for the arabica plant to thrive. The coffee bushes, which are combined with other crops, are grown beneath shady trees and fertilized organically. The coffee cherries produced are hand-picked and carefully sorted, before being processed using the wet method, with a fermentation time of 12 to 36 hours. This intricate orchestration of regional characteristics and harvesting techniques contribute to the unique profile of Bali's arabica coffee. GI certification serves to highlight these qualities, so that it may be distinguished as a superior coffee amongst distributors.

In this way, GI certification establishes a direct link between the distinct traits of a coffee and its geographical origin. By endorsing a coffee product with a government-issued stamp, the origins and locally developed standards of that coffee are guaranteed to consumers everywhere. GIs also have the potential to deliver intangible benefits related to regional pride and social identity. This form of symbolic branding asserts a moral claim over the geographical and cultural property embodied by a coffee and helps to support and preserve Bali's cultural traditions—an outcome that organic and Fairtrade initiatives specifically aim to achieve.

Long before the emergence of ethical buzz words like Fairtrade and organic took hold in the realm of coffee producers, agricultural practices centered on environmental sustainability, ecological conservation, and ethical production, were well-established in Bali. A deep, spiritual reverence for the natural environment has guided the ethics and sustainability of coffee cultivation in the region for centuries. Origin stories, which often borrow from the cultural and geographical imagery of Bali's coffee producing regions create an engaging narrative. It's one of authenticity that appeals to the imagination of consumers, with vivid descriptions of their cup of arabica coffee being sourced from organically grown beans, hand-picked from the rugged slopes of an ancient volcano, nestled in the exotic highlands of Bali.

—

Nature Dreams and Beans

WORDS Nicholas O'Hara-Boyd
ILLUSTRATION Lauren Rebbeck

After a particularly long and stressful year—a messy break-up with a long-time lover, a sudden health crisis, and a hectic job in inner-city London that kept me wired around the clock—I needed an escape. I needed to swim, explore, climb. I needed to get back to nature. That would be the healing my soul needed; that would be my medicine.

Of course, as a coffee lover, this land of blissful fantasy would have to include some of the finest beans the world has to offer. But did such a place exist?

Bali has a reputation as being the Cancun of the Southern Hemisphere—hot, wet and wild. But once you escape the explosive EDM sets, happy hour cocktails, and swarms of young tourists free of inhibitions, there's a far more peaceful, wholesome, and holistic side to this corner of Indonesia.

Largely unspoiled, this island paradise is home to some of the most stunning natural wonders of the world. From volcanoes and waterfalls to beaches and forests, Bali promised the soul-soothing getaway I needed.

Click. Flight booked. I was going.

The melodrama of a twentysomething hitting quarter-life crisis isn't lost on me. But in today's burnout culture, perhaps it's a little more understandable than it once was. In my search for detox from the madness of the West, Elizabeth Gilbert's 2006 memoir *Eat Pray Love* served as a liberation inspiration.

Perhaps for this reason, Padang Padang Beach, an iconic location within her story, was my first stop. One of Bali's best-known seaside strips and home to the Rip Curl Cup, its golden sand and limestone cliffs make it one of the most stunning places on the island to have a paddle and cool

down. As the sun beamed upon my shoulders and the waves lapped at my feet, I smiled. This is what I was craving.

A short stroll from the beach, I happened upon The Mango Tree Cafe. Dotted with Buddhas and lined with gorgeous cobblestone, perhaps the most impressive thing about it is its namesake. Towering over the cafe's courtyard, a mango tree's luscious branches shaded me while I enjoyed a cup of *kopi* with beans roasted on site and sourced from local organic farms in the nearby mountains. It was as rich and chocolatey as I could have hoped.

For years, one of my favourite relaxation rituals has been to crack open a beer, put on a Miles Davis record and watch an old '70s surf film. There's something mesmerising about watching bronzed bodies balancing on planks as they dance across a break in a rhythmic battle with the ocean.

It was this that had me so excited about the big waves of Blue Point, Suluban Beach, one of the finest spots in Bali to watch surfers young and old carve up the swell. What I wasn't expecting, however, was something even more spectacular right next door.

Accessible only by foot, the caves off Suluban Beach team with hundreds of little nooks and crannies, splattered with shards of daylight. Getting lost in them, and weaving out of the maze, makes for a perfect afternoon adventure. Luckily, I arrived at sunset and low tide, which made for easy access and the best photographs.

Within the hour I was sipping a warm cup of java at the nearby Suka Espresso. An old *warung* turned hip and fresh cafe, the aroma of the beans wafting in the ocean breeze was enough to lure me in as if I was a cartoon character smelling a cherry pie on a windowsill. It certainly didn't disappoint.

Already feeling more myself than I had in months, the next day I decided on a change of pace—it was time to get the blood pumping.

There's a very good reason that anyone you talk to seems to agree that a climb up the top of Gunung Batur is essential if you're visiting the region. The unparalleled views over the sea and forests from this active volcano are worth the sweat you'll work up as you weave your way to the top. If you want to get some fresh air into your lungs, at 1,717 meters, you won't find purer.

Predicting that I'd need a little extra energy before embarking on the pilgrimage, I made a brief stop off at Kintamani Eco Bike Coffee. With a spectacular vista of the mountain, this coffee shop and roaster was the ideal place to experience the best local beans on offer. Its Cobra blend is perhaps their most beloved—fruity and floral. It was my weapon of choice and, if the way I proceeded to shoot up that mountain is anything to go off, a needed pre-climb boost.

After ascending a mountain, there's no better way to cool off than with a shower. And this tropical nirvana can do one better—a waterfall shower. At Sekumpul, that is exactly what I found.

Eighty metres up in the middle of a lush bamboo forest, a cluster of half a dozen cascades is one of the most striking waterfalls this island boasts. As I wound my way down toward the rock pools, I even passed a couple of coffee plantations. Feeling cheeky, I plucked a cherry and saw firsthand why these coffee trees are consistently regarded as some of the finest in the world. The smell alone will make you salivate.

From this bamboo forest, I took off to another one of the most beautiful pockets of luscious rainforest on Bali. Between its paddy and marigold fields, cocoa trees and scenic views, the vast forest of Sambangan feels untouched. Full of waterfalls and native wildlife, you'd be hard-pressed to find anywhere more tranquil on the island. For me it was the perfect place to end my forage for freedom.

It doesn't get any more authentic than the family-run Waroeng Noceng, a small restaurant within driving distance of the Sambangan Gorge. While being smack-bang in the middle of a forest means that it's harder to find a cup of joe that will leave you enraptured, one thing that can be promised here is a memorable experience. Sitting among the locals who, even if they can't speak your language, will happily communicate with a sea of wide-eyed grins, will remain with you for a lifetime.

For the first time in a long time I felt a real connection—both with the people and the land they call their home. I felt rejuvenated. I felt replenished. I felt ready to start over fresh.

If you want to find a little peace and quiet at the bottom of a coffee cup, Bali is your mecca. Whether you're exploring caves, hiking a mountain or swimming in glistening waters, you're bound to find a unique caffeine haven nearby serving celebrated Balinese *kopi* delicacies. With most sourcing local, organic beans and roasting onsite, you're almost always promised a wide range of new and exciting flavours.

Erupting with heart and soul, if Bali isn't the paradise that can bring you back to life, I don't know what is.

—

Waroeng Noceng

BLUE POINT

PADANG PADANG BEACH

SULUBAN BEACH CAVES

SEKUMPUL

GUNUNG BATUR

Kintamani Eco
Bike Coffee

-UBUD-

DENPASAR

The
Mango Cafe

Suka Espresso

It's Time for Farmers to Drink Specialty Coffee Too

WORDS Michelle Anindya
PHOTOGRAPHS Tino Renato

Across Indonesia, one of the greatest hindrances to introducing the principles of specialty coffee is that the farmers rarely—if ever—get to taste the distinct flavors of specialty coffee.

For most coffee farmers in Indonesia, *kopi jagung* (coffee roasted with corn kernels), the deep, full-bodied aromatic drink heaped with sugar, is still the perfect cup of seduction. 'It tastes like tea' is generally the first impression this manually-brewed single origin coffee gives.

Yet this is changing, as specialty coffee shops are entering deeper into the rural areas and closer to the farmers' homes—there's one "a 15-minute walk from my house," according to a coffee farmer in Kintamani. This specialty coffee shop, with its balcony facing the lofty and majestic Mount Batur, with coffee growing at its foothills, is Kintamani Eco Bike Coffee.

Located in the northern highlands of Bali, Kintamani is the famed coffee district that spans 48 villages. It is surrounded by Bali's sacred mountains, lush jungles, and secret waterfalls.

"Our roastery is just next door, the processor is our neighbor, and the farm is located in a village across [from] the coffee shop," said Wahyuni Indriawati, owner and house manager of Kintamani Eco Bike Coffee. As a coffee producing region, Bali is rather unusual. You could be hopping coffee shops in the Melbourne-like district of Canggu in the morning, meeting a local roaster with over 20 years of experience by noon, then chatting with coffee farmers from Kintamani in the afternoon. Short meet-ups lead to longer meetings, coffee farm visits lead to partnerships—proximity is what keeps the scene brewing hot. Indriawati and her husband, I Gusti Agung Djelantik Bayusutha, or Bayu for short, hopped on the coffee's third wave in 2014, before immersing themselves into the entire process of coffee making, from *hulu* to *hilir*—from crop to cup.

Even though having control at all stages in the coffee-making process is many coffee shop owners' dream, it is one thing to be a coffee farmer or processor, and another to be a coffee shop owner.

A common annoyance to roasters around the world is that the green beans that arrive don't match the samples. However in Bali, with the farmers living minutes away from the coffee shop, collaborative work with them is not impossible, it's intuitive.

"The first thing that we asked from farmers was *petik merah saja* (red picks only)," said Wahyuni. This hand-picked red cherry, by the specialty standards, is the proper indication that the beans are mature enough for processing.

Many coffee farmers in Bali, after decades of selling commercial grade coffee beans that end up as instant coffee, are accustomed to strip-picking coffee cherries in all sorts of colors and stages of maturity: green, yellow, orange, red. Since they are not paid by quality, but per kilo, the faster they bag a kilo of cherries, the faster they earn the money. Instead of picking the ripe, ruby-red cherries, bagging them in all sorts of colors is the most expedient thing to do.

Maha Wiguna, Kintamani Eco Bike Coffee

"And this happens everywhere," added Wahyuni, "including in the Batur area, which is new to the concept of specialty coffee. We are possibly the only specialty processor in Batur."

Wahyuni and Bayu, thankfully, also live around the coffee farm, so befriending neighbors and farmers is a natural thing to do. After a series of fruitful business encounters with local residents and farmers, Wahyuni and Bayu invited them to Kintamani Eco Bike Coffee for a conversation about coffee cherries. Comparing the yellow, orange, and red cherries, Bayu showed the farmers that the ripe red cherries are the ones that contain the fullest potential, the prized commodity. "Not yellow, not orange," added Bayu.

Every year, Bayu gives thousands of coffee seeds to the farmers. These seeds are supposed to be more resilient and resistant to diseases, which saves farmers time, energy, and money. Yet, even with financial incentives, it takes time to break decades of bad habits.

Most, if not all, coffee farmers don't drink specialty coffee—even though they are the ones who grow it. The common story of "the good ones are for export and the bad ones are for domestic consumption" still holds true. When the market changes its taste preferences for coffee, farmers are the last ones to know about it. Communicating these flavor profiles—what is currently trending in the market—has always been a problem because farmers lack the references.

At the Batur Temple, one of Bali's most sacred temples facing the majestic Mount Agung, Bali's highest mountain, Bayu has been giving away coffee drinks to local visitors to show them the potential of their own produce. For many of them, it's the first time that they've experienced their own, regional coffee roasted to maximize its flavors. The reactions have been varied, but knowing that there is a new market for higher quality beans gives them a sense of identity and hope for the future of specialty coffee in their own region. "The key is patience and building a sense of community," said Bayu.

That is why a specialty coffee shop in a coffee growing region makes a difference. It speeds up the feedback loop, stimulates the local economy, and breaks boundaries within the extensive supply chain bureaucracy. When farmers learn the value of the coffee they produce— even better, when they can see the burgeoning market themselves—they understand the destination, the goal. And it encourages them to produce better product.

With Mount Batur rising in the distance, at Kintamani Eco Bike Coffee, local Indonesians who drive two hours from Denpasar enjoy a cup of coffee grown just a few minutes away. Wahyuni and Bayu don't need a glistening photo of a coffee farmer gently grasping a bunch of red cherries hanging in their coffee shop, their farmer and processor visit the coffee shop often, tasting their coffee. "I drink good coffee every day now. Our own coffee," they said.

—

A Pledge to Sustainability

WORDS Kayleigh Rattle
PHOTOGRAPHS Adam Goldberg, Daniela Velasco

Bali's beauty and allure have attracted tourists for decades, and with good reason: with its verdant rice paddies, golden beaches, coral-filled seas, and outstanding natural biodiversity, Bali is—for many—as close as it gets to paradise. But such attractions and charm, on top of bringing in more than six million visitors a year (up to 80% of the island's economy now relies on tourism) has also created a very problematic by-product: waste. And, in particular, plastic.

Bali reportedly produces more than 3,500 tonnes of rubbish a day, with just over half of that actually reaching landfill sites. Not only that, but Indonesia is thought to be the second largest contributor to ocean plastic in the world, after China. Numbers aside, the environmental impacts of such a colossal scale of waste are not only striking, but also easily observed today. Even if you haven't ventured to Bali recently, chances are you will have seen—or at least heard of—British diver Rich Horner and his eye-opening underwater video from 2018. The footage captures a sea of plastic bags and detritus floating around him off the coast of Bali. With barely a fish to be seen amongst the debris, the video unsurprisingly went viral, and has ultimately helped to raise awareness of Bali's plastic waste problem globally.

But how can this crisis be alleviated? The Balinese government officially recognises the island's plastic problem—something that of course is prevalent worldwide, and not just relevant to Indonesia—and introduced a ban on single-use plastics, such as shopping bags, Styrofoam, and straws in December of 2018. Discussions are also currently underway regarding the possible introduction of a tourist tax, the revenue of which would go towards preserving the Balinese culture and its environment, which could help reduce the island's plastic problem, and ultimately clean up its once-pristine waters and beaches.

But it's not just the government's responsibility; protecting Bali also falls on residents and business owners—and, undoubtedly, the island's

Revive Cafe

visitors. One particular area of Balinese society that seems to be taking an active approach to tackling waste and sustainability is Bali's thriving coffee sector. From forgoing plastic straws to serving iced coffee in glass bottles, and even banning takeaways altogether, many of the island's bean-loving baristas, coffee shops, cafes, and roasters are doing what they can to reduce their ecological footprint.

One such example is Ombak Zero Waste Cafe on Jungut Batu Bay on the Balinese island of Nusa Lembongan, to the southeast of Bali. As owner Nagi Nurwulan explains, the cafe "aims to get as close to generating no waste as possible, in order to keep this island beautiful." This includes eliminating single-use plastic items; composting organic waste; feeding animals such as chickens, ducks, cows, and pigs food waste; purchasing directly from suppliers to avoid unnecessary packaging; and recycling plastic bottles and containers.

"There are so many initiatives happening all over Bali to tackle its waste and pollution problem," Nurwulan tells us. "However, we need more people on board because the waste problem is growing at a much faster rate than ever before." One way he plans to raise consciousness and educate customers is by putting a stop to disposable coffee cups altogether. "We only serve our coffee in-house, and do not offer takeaway cups in a bid to reduce waste. We are happy to serve customers who bring their own takeaway containers," explains Nurwulan. Keeping it local, Nagi sources coffee beans directly from a local supplier, who roasts them in-house. Nurwulan also takes his own containers with him to collect the beans to circumvent any of the superfluous packaging.

Workin g directly with suppliers to reduce waste and packaging is also something close to the heart of Prawira Adhiguna, who everyone calls "Edo." Edo runs Hungry Bird Coffee Roastery out of Canggu, close to holiday hotspot Seminyak. "As a coffee roastery, we deliver coffee to our Balinese clients by using reusable buckets instead of plastic packaging. All of our milk carton packaging gets picked up by a local recycling company, too," explains Edo. In addition, Hungry Bird endeavours to use local coffee to reduce its carbon footprint. It has also replaced plastic straws with stainless steel straws, rewards customers who bring in their own tumblers with a discount, and turns any unused coffee grounds into compost. "If you're comparing Bali to more developed countries, we still have a long way to go," says Edo. "However, as the first and only province in Indonesia to legally ban single-use plastic, Styrofoam, and many more synthetic materials, Bali is definitely turning heads. So much so, Bali's plastic ban, implemented [in] December [of] 2018, is now being applied in Jakarta. I'm proud to say my cafe is located in an area where the community is so involved in this movement, which has been incredibly refreshing to witness."

For general manager Oliver Broughton, who runs Revive Bali in Ubud's Penestanan Village, the relationship between coffee and sustainability is something deeply ingrained within the culture of the cafe, as well as the wider community. "We're definitely seeing a slow and steady progress in terms of Bali managing its waste pollution problem. A big step being the ban on plastic bags—a great move!" Broughton tells us. "As a cafe, what we find inspiring are the individuals who take initiative and rally hard to start sustainable projects." One such project is the "Forest Smoothie" movement, the world's first cafe conservation project, and something Revive Bali strongly supports. "A frequent customer, and a dear friend of ours, collects a percentage of profits from our green smoothies, and then uses this revenue to tackle deforestation in Indonesia—he literally gathers other wildlife warriors and locals bi-monthly to plant thousands of trees."

On top of supporting such pioneering projects from its customer base and community, the cafe tries to use minimal plastic. "One of our boldest choices would have to be the decision to not use takeaway coffee cups," explains Broughton. "After reading up on the greenwashing of so-called 'sustainable' coffee cups—and how 99.99% of these cups in Bali will never make it to its proper recycling plant to break down or biodegrade properly—we proudly do not offer takeaways. It's actually nice, as it gives the customer five minutes or so to themselves to drink inside, connect with other people, and to just catch a breath."

Indeed, could this ritual of simply taking a moment to connect with others, and "catching a breath" be just the approach that needs to be adopted to continue to solve Bali's—and the world's—waste problem? Life is already far too disposable, and living is far too fast. Perhaps if we all took a moment to slow down a little, and to drink our coffee mindfully like Broughton, we'd start to take notice of—and fully appreciate—not only the beautiful island of Bali we're lucky enough to be able to visit, but also the planet on which we live. There certainly is no better time to wake up and smell the coffee.

—

The Ugly Truth Behind Bali's Civet Poop Coffee

WORDS Anita Surewicz
PHOTOGRAPHS Adam Goldberg, Daniela Velasco

Some of the most expensive coffee in the world comes from the Indonesian islands of Bali, Sulawesi, Sumatra, Sumba, and Flores. Popular among coffee aficionados across the world, *kopi luwak*, sometimes also referred to as poop coffee, is produced from coffee cherries that have been partially digested by Asian palm civets. The enzymes in the digestive tract of the critters, locally known as *luwak*, are said to seep through the beans as they ferment, removing some of the acidity inherent in coffee. While the production of *kopi luwak* on the holiday island of Bali is relatively small compared to the rest of the archipelago, it has made a huge contribution to popularizing the brew internationally and changing the face of the industry. Each day, throngs of tourists visit the island's *kopi luwak* plantations to sample the brew and buy it for their loved ones back home. Little do they know that behind their cup of coffee lies a cruel industry that is taking its toll on the cuddly-looking animals.

Kopi luwak was traditionally sourced from the droppings of wild civets, which were gathered from the forest floor and sold to roasters. In fact, the practice originated in the 18th century with Indonesian workers on Dutch plantations, who were forbidden from picking coffee for themselves. The farmers started to scavenge beans from civet droppings, and soon realized that after being cleaned and roasted they made a surprisingly smooth cup of coffee. Over the years, this time-consuming way of harvesting the undigested beans, however, has given way to a battery cage system where civets are force-fed coffee cherries for months at a time, only to die after a shortened life of pain and disease. This has been mainly due to the increasing demand created by tourists, who take home holiday stories, and coffee beans, from destinations such as Bali.

The walls of coffee emporiums are not adorned in behind-the-scenes photographs of *kopi luwak* production, where civets are stacked in tiny cages, as the ugly reality of farmed *kopi luwak* does not sell coffee. Tracy Wilkinson, who has been rescuing infant civets in Bali for the past four years, and hopes to one day open a *luwak* sanctuary on the island, says that tourists visiting *kopi luwak* plantations are rarely exposed to the ugly truth behind the product. "The civets can appear healthy and content, snoozing in cages under shady trees. However, they are nocturnal, sleeping most of the day and highly active at night," Wilkinson says. "Tourists don't see the extreme stress, the frenetic pacing and the heartbreaking crying of a trapped civet. They don't see them when they

have deformed feet and open wounds from trying to push through the wire cages to freedom. They certainly don't notice that their teeth have been cut and they are often de-clawed so they don't bite or scratch a tourist."

Virtually all *kopi luwak* in Bali comes from caged civets, and as the industry is unregulated even coffee labeled "wild" is unlikely to be the real deal. The practice of using civets for coffee production is not only cruel, but results in an inferior product. In the wild, civets feast on a diet of ripe coffee cherries, as well as insects, reptiles and other fruit. Caged civets, on the other hand, are force-fed run-of-the-mill cherries and lack the required variety in their diet, which often leads to malnutrition and disease. "Indonesia has weak farmer organization, high variation in production systems and limited government support. As such, how could any standards be communicated to farmers, let alone enforced," Wilkinson asks. "This lack of ethical standards for farming and production practices leaves the sector vulnerable to mistruths and questionable marketing strategies, pushing the onus of integrity and fairness of trade on the buyer, not the seller."

Even though finding ethical *kopi luwak* in Bali might be a distant dream at the moment, coffee connoisseurs should not hesitate to visit one of Bali's coffee plantations that does not produce the product. As most of Bali's coffee is grown by small landholders, this goes a long way to supporting ventures that are engaged in ethical behavior. "These farming families derive a modest living from the production of coffee, distinct from the tiny and often corrupt market for *kopi luwak*," Wilkinson says. "If you really have to visit a *kopi luwak* production facility, I would do extensive research to uncover where the coffee berries are grown and how the civet poop is collected. Without at least photographic evidence of the coffee plantations and the jungles surrounding them that provide habitat to wild civets eating the berries, I would not entertain tasting or buying *kopi luwak* from a tourist attraction."

The only way that change can take place is by encouraging demand for authentic *kopi luwak* sourced from wild civets and declining to purchase coffee beans that are the end product of irresponsible practices. There are already foundations in Bali that work with villages and communities to develop tourism around eco-farming. *Kopi luwak* production could fit into this model. Wilkinson's dream to one day establish a civet sanctuary that also funds farmer education and ethical coffee production is a case in point. "We should be encouraging farmers and producers to examine their processes and practices, and search for more responsible ways to derive fair income and sustainable lifestyles. Bali could serve as a model for other Indonesian coffee producing islands and facilitate real change," Wilkinson says. "I am optimistic. Once upon a time, we did not consider the plight of battery hens producing eggs in atrocious conditions. Now, we ask for organic, free-range, and barn-raised egg production. If it is possible for chickens to get free, this is also possible for civets."

—

Origin at Origin:
Q&A with Rodney Glick,
Owner of Seniman Coffee

INTRODUCTION Thomas Wensma
INTERVIEW & PHOTOGRAPHS Adam Goldberg, Daniela Velasco

Australian born Rodney Glick came to Bali with an intent to do wood carving. Instead, he started trading coffee. This led the contemporary artist into starting Seniman Coffee.

In the past five years, Indonesia, like other coffee-growing countries, has seen the rise of what Glick calls the "fourth wave" of coffee, driven by growing domestic interest, consumption, and research in coffee. In Bali, the fourth wave has bridged the local coffee-producing culture with the global standards of coffee processing and education that have developed abroad. And to that end, Glick has helped to bring knowledge and context to the Bali coffee scene, and developed adaptive tools and solutions for local coffee producers and baristas to access those global standards.

Rodney Glick

Seniman Coffee

Where are we right now?
We're sitting in the middle of rice fields. But we are in a coffee processing facility outside of Ubud.

Is this considered a suburb?
It's a village, and Ubud is the center. Around Ubud are multiple villages. Traditionally, each of these villages surrounding this center were specialized in some sort of craft, especially around Ubud. Right now we are in what was traditionally a wood carving area. There are other villages that specialize in jewelry, ceramics, or painting. I mean that's traditionally how the villages worked.

Your partner Kadek Edi mentioned that he was a woodcarver until he got into coffee.
Yes, because that's how the villages functioned, from the grandfather to the father to the kids, and they would learn craft by action.

Are you originally from Australia?
Yes, but well-educated, hah.

I came to Bali in 2005 intending to do wood carving. By profession, I'm a contemporary artist. But at the same time, I started trading robusta [coffee]. I still have a wood carving practice, but I've stopped exhibiting.

How would you summarize specialty coffee in Ubud or Bali right now?
Well, they're feeding off of what's happening everywhere in the world and so what started as a focus on origin in non-coffee growing countries is turning into a focus on the people who actually grow the stuff and then process the stuff themselves.

What's motivating this push?
The middle class. It created desire for agricultural products. Many have studied overseas or spent time overseas and saw the coffee situation abroad and then realized that "well, we're in a coffee-growing country… we can also grow and we can also roast and we can also drink our own coffee." And especially in Indonesia, the last five years have seen that push.

The whole coffee growing belt is experiencing growth. From the Tropic of Capricorn to the Tropic of Cancer. That's Central America, Africa, the whole of Asia. You get the whole of India. And in China, you've got two billion more people interested in that product. Mexico is also big. So you've got a homegrown demand, whereas before, the structure was "grow it and send it out," because the domestic markets were not able to afford those products. But if you have a big middle class—I mean which is what has happened in Indonesia, a country of 250 million people— then you have a domestic market for a domestic product.

Are you seeing more domestic consumption as opposed to exports?
Yes. That is definitely growing. Last year was the first year [Seniman Coffee's head roaster Kadek] Edi and I could choose between exporting or selling to the rest of the domestic market. The price is slightly different but not a lot anymore. It was always an option, but no one domestically was that interested in specialty. But that has completely changed. Five years ago on the board of the shop, we would always have to have four or five origins outside of Indonesia—Africa, Panama, Mexico, whatever. The origins didn't really matter except you had to have a spread to be seen as a specialty coffee shop to the domestic customer. The domestic customer would want to taste other origins. And now, if you look on our board, we don't have to have any. The domestic market no longer wants to come into our shop and say, "I want an Ethiopian, I want a Panamanian, I want a Mexican coffee." They're only interested in Indonesian coffee because Indonesia grows a lot of coffee in a lot of different climates and in lots of different geographical areas.

When we were in the roastery, I noticed what I thought was an SCAA color wheel. But when I looked closely, it had Indonesian fruit references.

I used to read about coffee, and I used to think: these people don't live in coffee-growing countries! They live in America, Australia, Europe—but no one's growing coffee there. And the idea of the third wave of coffee came from these places, right? And I read the writings about what the next wave will be, and it was usually focused on customer experience; technology is next, also design and architecture. It was about a shift in the coffee shop.

I mean, if you're not in a coffee-growing country that's what you see, right? You don't see origin. What you see is, "Wow that's a new machine, and this is a new under-counter espresso maker, and that's a modbar, and everything's just so hip and cool." There's a lot of theater.

I first wrote about the fourth wave with that in mind. I realized that the fourth wave is actually not about the places where the third wave took place. The focus has shifted. But no one in the places where third wave took place wants to hear that the focus has shifted. Because, if the focus has shifted to coffee-growing countries, that means they're not included in the fourth wave. Well, they are. There are ramifications—the price of coffee is going to change, the export market is going to change, the demand is going to change. That is exactly what has been happening.

So fourth wave coffee is…?

Coffee-growing countries that start to focus on their own coffee, or, the focus on origin at origin: that's fourth wave. And it is happening everywhere. You go to India, you go to Thailand, come here, go to Mexico, go to parts of Africa, Brazil, and Colombia—there's an energy in these places because there's an educated middle class that celebrates its national agricultural products, like coffee. So there's a bit of nationalism that drives this wave, but also money.

And the tasting wheel is a part of it?

I recognize the benefits of having one standard wheel that the whole world uses. So that someone in Africa, or Bali, or the United States, can have the same point of reference.

At the same time, it's a matter of practicality. If you have baristas or coffee people trying to get accreditation, [the accreditation] is coming from America, or was. So if you want to be a Q grader or a Q processor or whatever the degrees are, the [tests] rely on an aroma and flavor wheel developed in America. And when you're in [Indonesia], it's totally alien. It's out of context and has no relevance to [Indonesians]. So if you want someone from Indonesia to understand, let's just change the wheel. Not the structure, but rather, make references to local flavors and local tastes.

How has the reception been to the Indonesian tasting wheel?

Fantastic. We released the first draft for one month and asked for feedback, and released the revised one in April. For the final one, it was available in PDF format for download. I think there have been more than 10,000 downloads.

I can see it when the young kids are trying to describe coffee. They no longer have to reference something that has no meaning [to them]. You can see it in the cupping lab. They point to the board and know exactly what the references are. It's immediate. So I think that's good.

And do you think other coffee-growing countries are going to start putting together their own?

Absolutely. Look at Taiwan. It's just ahead of us actually. At the same time they released their own version of the wheel full of local fruits and local references.

Do you ever use the original SCAA wheel?

Realistically, we use both wheels. As you see in our cupping lab, we have both because you have to know the reference of where it comes from. We're not trashing the original wheel. What we're trying to do is help—nearly every barista that we have comes from villages around here, did not finish high school, has had no coffee education. So how do they begin to understand what the hell we're talking about? Especially to a customer who's sitting in front of them with whom they might want to discuss single origin. So it's a tool to integrate into their own experience.

From a coffee growing standpoint, Bali seems quite diverse….

Except, it doesn't have high altitude. Not like places like Flores, Papua, or Bandung, or Java.

Also, up until recently, the government pushed out varieties of arabica [coffee] all across the archipelago, including Bali. Sadly, they were developed for fecundity, not for flavor.

What's dynamic about Bali's coffee scene?

The strength of Bali is not just that it has domestic tourism but it has international tourism. So you get this mega-cultural mix of people from around the world coming to this tiny little place. The mix of people in a cafe on any given day is incredible. That's not typical of the whole of Indonesia.

There are a lot of coffee people too—a lot of them on holiday. And that generates a range of discussion. So I think the good thing with Bali is there's a lot of global input about coffee, which leads to processes like carbonic maceration, for example. In the last two, three years, there has been an explosion in coffee processing because of conversations and cross-pollination of ideas. And Bali's part of that because of the cultural mix you'll find here, which doesn't really exist elsewhere.

—

Flavors of Process:
Q&A with Kadek Edi,
Q Grader and Head Roaster at Seniman Coffee

INTRODUCTION Thomas Wensma
INTERVIEW & PHOTOGRAPHS Adam Goldberg, Daniela Velasco

Like Rodney Glick, his business partner at Seniman Coffee, head roaster Kadek Edi used to be a woodcarver. Overcoming his father's expectations, he started working in coffee. Wanting to learn how to properly grade and process coffee led him on a path to become Bali's first and only Q grader in 2013. It's the highest accreditation for a green coffee evaluation expert. Within the rigorous training one must pass 19 tests, that include triangulation, cupping, olfactory tests, roasted grading, green coffee grading, and sensory skills, among others. Based on an agreed language of quality in processing and sensory analysis, it results in a globally shared standard for buyers, traders, roasters and other coffee professionals alike. Here, Edi shares the intricacies of coffee processing methods and how these influence the flavor characteristics of Balinese specialty coffee.

Kadek Edi

Tell us a little about you.

My name is Kadek Edi. I'm from Kubu, Bali, and I'm the head roaster at Seniman Coffee. I started roasting professionally in 2014. Recently, I was a finalist in the COE, or Cup of Excellence. I just won that three months ago. And I'm the first Q grader from Bali.

What flavor characteristics of Balinese coffee do you like?

Well, with Balinese coffee, people say the flavor has notes of orange and citrus, because where the coffee crops are grown there are many orange trees. But in my opinion it has nothing to do with the orange trees. More likely, I think it's because of the natural fermentation process. During fermentation, enzymes ferment the coffee increasing the acidity. The longer the coffee ferments, the higher the acidity.

Is Balinese coffee fermented longer than other coffees?

The natural coffee that we process here is fermented longer, but generally it depends on the taste we are aiming for. Some coffee drinkers want higher acidity. We have our washed process, we have our honey process and we have our natural process. The natural process fermentation takes longer—because the beans slowly dry in the sun, taking more time. This longer fermentation creates a very strong, citrus fruit taste. With washed process coffee on the other hand, you just pop the coffee bean from the cherry and put it in a fermentation tank for 24 hours, then rinse it. This is a much shorter fermentation, so it yields a less acidic coffee. And lastly our honey process coffee comes out more caramelized—it has more sweetness, more mellow, milder flavors.

Could you describe the difference between natural, honey, and washed process?

With our natural process coffee, we simply sort and let the coffee dry in the sun. We rake the beans and turn them to facilitate the drying. Sometimes it takes up to a month to fully dry. There is a lot of fermentation, so the flavor could be strong and more fruity.

The honey process is similar to the natural process, with a few differences. First, we immerse the cherries in water so the defective ones float to the top. Then we remove the cherry skin and pulp, leaving behind some of the mucilage. After that, we let it dry just like the natural process. It's a little sticky on the surface, like honey.

With the washed process, the coffee cherries are washed in water until the skin and pulp are removed. Then, the beans are put in a fermentation tank for 24 hours. Some facilities do 36 hours, depending on the taste you're looking for.

Can you tell us a little bit about Q grading here?

I wanted to become a Q grader because I wanted to learn how to properly grade and process coffee. It's very useful for a farmer, for an exporter, and for a coffee roaster. Because I am a coffee roaster, it's a useful skill [to be able to] discern between good and bad coffees. How else can you identify defects and learn how to remove them? It was also helpful to learn how to describe the flavors and aromas in coffee. Especially describing the taste after roasting—how do different roasts affect the flavor? And then getting into blending—if different coffees have a different roast level, what happens if you mix them? If you want to have more acidity, you add more natural process coffee… if you want to make a blend less acidic, you take out the natural coffee and add more honey, or more washed process. Things like that were helpful to learn.

Did you drink coffee growing up in Kubu? Do you remember the first time you drank it?

Yeah, like since I was a kid. I think the first time was when I was in elementary school because I distinctly remember watching my dad drink it and thinking that I wanted to drink it, too. We grew up with robusta coffee.

Nyoman Patra

Commodity coffee?

Yeah. Also very finely ground. We grew up drinking coffee like that so we got used to the strong earthy flavors. I think most people in Bali got used to getting sweetness from adding sugar and not from the coffee itself.

Do you think Indonesians are changing their expectations of what coffee tastes like because of specialty coffee in Bali?

Yes.

Would your dad drink this specialty coffee?

I got my dad to try the specialty coffee I produce as soon as I started working here. I think he likes my coffee because he stopped drinking robusta. He even started drinking coffee without sugar.

Was it hard for him to adjust?

I don't think so. It goes like this: when you're a parent… and your son is doing something and it becomes a big success, you're proud and tell everyone "my kid has great coffee." He's especially proud because he's the one who enabled it. Before I got involved with coffee, my career was wood carving. My father expected me to become a wood carver. When I told my father I wasn't going to carve wood, and instead, was going to get involved with coffee, he thought it was very unusual and said, "What exactly are you doing in coffee? Coffee won't make you rich." And then when I started to work in coffee, my dad became very disappointed. He wanted me to work in hospitality and I said no. I was arguing with him a lot, and there were times when I wouldn't talk to him. Coffee? He just couldn't believe it. Because in Bali the price of coffee was around one cent per cup. How are you going to make money for the family, he wondered? I just wanted to do something deeper in value. I said one day, one day. Yes, my family was a bit harsh with me. It was hard to control me because I wanted to do something different from what my parents expected. But now, coffee is everywhere.

What's your favorite part of Q grading?

I meet a lot of interesting people and am constantly learning from them. At first I didn't care if I passed [the Q grader test] or not, I just wanted to learn from being there. That was my goal.

What's your favorite coffee in Indonesia?

Of course *my* coffee! The natural process one.

Natural from Kintamani?

Yes, I like it. But you know, the coffee from Papua is also unique. It's a mountainous island and the altitude is very high. The coffee never looks that good, but it almost always tastes very good. If you profile the roast correctly, the coffee comes out really good. It's a little tricky to get coffee from there, the access, the logistics and all that… but if you ask me without condition, "what's your favorite coffee in Indonesia?" My favorite is from Papua.

—

The Fourth Wave

WORDS Anita Surewicz
ILLUSTRATION provided by Seniman Coffee

The popular interpretation of the first three waves of coffee does not mention the involvement of coffee-growing countries. In fact, the concept of coffee waves has been derived from a Western perspective of world coffee trends, with regions such as the U.S.A., Europe, and Japan shaping the narrative around the beverage. With the people at the source now also drinking and experimenting with the brew, the fourth wave is here—and it is taking place in coffee-growing countries such as Indonesia. Beyond improvements in coffee quality and culinary appreciation, this direct participation of coffee-producing countries might just bring with it new clarity about the ill-defined idea of "direct trade" to provide transparency in all specialty coffee transactions, all the way to the consumer.

Coined by Trish Rothgeb, who first wrote about it in 2002, third wave coffee refers to a global movement where coffee production, from harvesting to brewing, focuses on bringing out the unique qualities of each bean. As the growing middle class in coffee-producing countries increasingly contemplates the quality of its own produce, however, it's also finding new pride in what is on offer. Rodney Glick, the Director of Coffee at Seniman Industries and Head of Innovation at Karana Global, a boutique coffee processor in Bali, says that it is this realization among locals, that domestically harvested beans can be just as good as imported beans, that is driving and shaping the fourth wave movement within coffee producing countries. "When a consumer drinks her own local coffee, she participates in the fourth wave, no matter if it is a Brazilian drinking Brazilian beans [in Brazil] or an Indonesian drinking Indonesian beans [in Indonesia]. Beyond the consumption, it's about acknowledging that locals have the capacity to shape and influence the national coffee culture," he says.

In Indonesia, the local coffee market is growing not just thanks to increasing disposable income, but also due to local knowledge. Indonesians who are farming, harvesting, roasting, and brewing coffee have a unique understanding of their product, a know-how that is giving birth to new flavors and ways of looking at coffee. To smooth the way for experimentation, businesses in Indonesian regions such as Bali, Jakarta, and Bandung are working closely with producers to change the dialogue around specialty coffee. According to Evan Gilman, the Creative Director at The Crown: Royal Coffee Lab & Tasting Room U.S.A., who has conducted extensive research with coffee industry players in Indonesia, fourth wave coffee is all about maintaining the quality of specialty coffee while freely sharing its methodology. "Once consumers begin to demand the sort of radical transparency that's becoming common in these specialty circles, most businesses will need to follow suit, just as they have with previous waves," Gilman says. "The current relationship of the consumer to coffee is that they're only buying the final product and drinking it. A fourth wave extension of this trend may include producers working with one another, meeting end consumers, and closing communication gaps in the supply chain."

Up to now, the terminology of coffee waves has been framed from a Western perspective to the exclusion of the countries that have been the suppliers of beans for hundreds of years. An example of this is the coffee flavor wheel created by the Specialty Coffee Association (SCA), which has been designed to give producers a common language to discuss coffee-related issues. Based entirely on Western flavor references, the wheel fails to provide Indonesian coffee professionals with a common language that would help them stay in charge of their own narrative. "When Indonesians use it, not only do they not understand the flavors listed but some of the items the wheel refers to don't even grow in Indonesia, such as pomegranate or raspberry," Glick says.

The Roda Rasa Kopi Indonesia, an SCA-based flavor wheel with domestic adaptations, has been developed by Seniman Coffee and 5758 Coffee Lab to help Indonesians within the coffee industry take charge of their own narrative. With 5,000 downloads within just a couple of weeks, the wheel uses the SCA format but adapts the flavor descriptions to fruit and spices that grow in Indonesia, such as jackfruit and snake fruit. As such, the wheel is a part of the fourth wave, where coffee-growing countries take ownership of their own stories, a move that is increasingly helping to put them on the global map.

While these are important first steps, more are needed to ensure that it is not just the voices of the privileged few that are heard. This may just be one of the challenges that the fourth wave has to tackle. According to Gilman, while a select few who are participating in the supply chain in Indonesia are starting to benefit from the enhanced communication and visibility that social media and other technologies offer, this is not the case for everybody involved in the industry. "Social media can certainly play the part of giving producers a mouthpiece. We mustn't forget that the medium has its limitations, however. Can we expect every producer in a country such as Indonesia to have access to a smartphone and internet?" asks Gilman. "How can we open up the conversation to those whose voices have been traditionally limited by colonialism, and later by socioeconomic constraints?"

It is the hope of many that the fourth wave will serve as an agent of change for coffee-producing countries, such as Indonesia, creating better national and international awareness of issues affecting coffee farmers. Topics such as changing climate, water conservation, market pricing and brewing styles are just some of the fourth wave ideas that are likely to be the subjects of conversation in third wave consuming countries. "If this is a wave driven by coffee-growing countries, it's time to pass them the microphone. As consumers, we should be listening to whatever issues they want to address and however they want to speak about coffee. Beyond awareness, we should act on the items they've brought to our attention. The first step to awareness is listening," Gilman says.

Domestic coffee consumption in Indonesia is projected to keep rising and possibly even exceed exports. Beyond awareness and acknowledgment, when Indonesians drink their own coffee, whether as specialty or traditional coffee, it is the domestic coffee industry that benefits. According to Glick, the fourth wave will gradually evolve and can take many directions as determined by locals who are producing the beverage. "If there is a fifth wave, it may be characterized by robusta [coffee]. We're seeing a surge in interest in fine robusta beans, especially due to the global climate change that is threatening arabica [coffee] farms worldwide. Robusta is a lot more resilient at various latitudes and is more likely to survive unpredictable weather. With these characteristics and prospects, we might see more fine robusta from countries such as Indonesia in the future."

—

RODA RASA KOPI INDONESIA

INDONESIA'S COFFEE FLAVOR WHEEL

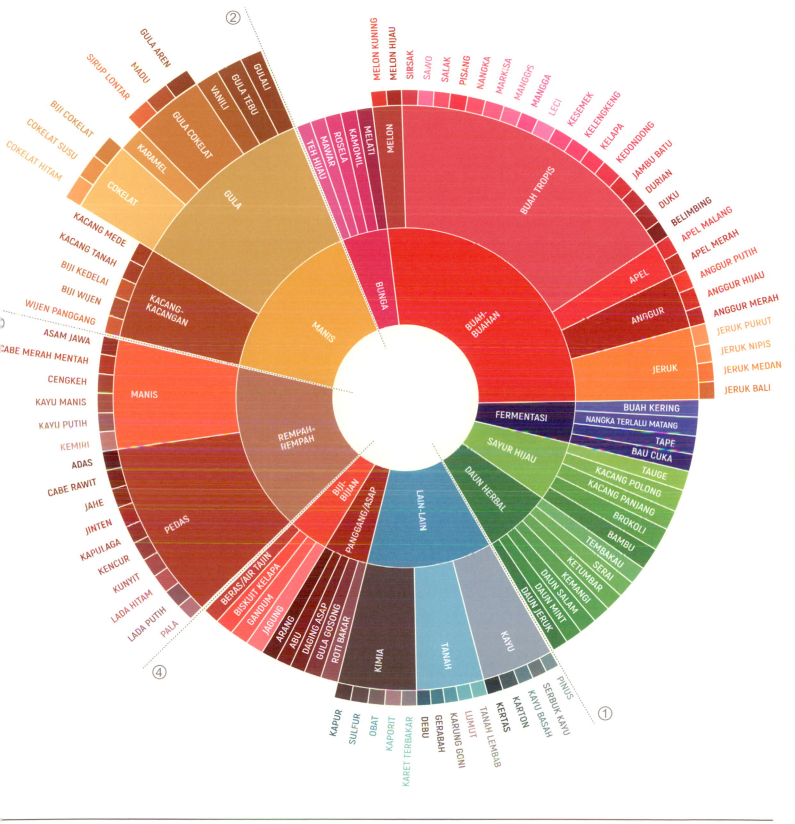

Fase Sangrai
1. Enzymatic
2. Sugar browning
3. Dry distillation
4. Aromatic taints

©2019

Intrinsically Indonesian

WORDS Ecky Prabanto
PHOTOGRAPHS Keng Pereira

I was born and raised in Indonesia. And in my years of living there, the archipelago nation has experienced an economic boom that has seen the expansion of many industries, including specialty coffee. A steep rise in domestic consumption of one of Indonesia's cash crops has helped accelerate the evolution of the Indonesian coffee community, creating a dynamic collection of baristas, farmers, processors, roasters, and cafes. And this growth and qualitative development could only have been achieved natively, with Indonesians working alongside Indonesians, from farm to cup. While it takes hundreds, if not thousands, of individuals to fully realize a supply chain, most of the world's coffee producing regions rely on exporting green coffee to consuming nations. By contrast, I believe Indonesia's internal consumption of coffee has created a "new" Indonesian specialty coffee scene, where direct communication in the native Bahasa tongue has connected Indonesian farmers with Indonesian baristas, and at every point in between.

While everyone involved with Indonesian coffee should be celebrated, a couple of figures emerge as exemplars of this ethos. Eko Purnomowidi is one. He's the co-founder of the farmer cooperative Klasik Beans and a self-described coffee socialist, he advocates for the even distribution of financial incentives to all involved in the organization. But Purnomowidi won't call himself a leader. He accepts his role as a communication centerpoint for Klasik Beans, a cooperative operating across every coffee producing island in Indonesia. Purnomowidi and the team's goals were to protect native soil while enriching the lives of people who work firsthand on the production of coffee. What started out 15 years ago as squatting on government owned mountainsides in West Java, deliberately disobeying the processing and harvesting "standards" of the Department of Agriculture in lieu of a more ecologically sustainable approach, has become a farming movement nationally. He credits the unique soil conditions, vegetation, and climate of Ethiopia for the rise of specialty coffee. So Klasik Bean's idea is to recreate the forest life of Ethiopia on the mountainsides of Indonesia. Using as many as 17 other agricultural plants that are native to both Indonesia and Ethiopia in order to propagate this concept, Purnomowidi's team has replanted hundreds of hectares of

mountainsides throughout Indonesia. Additionally, Purnomowidi developed a farming curriculum to spread his philosophy to all levels of the supply chain in Bahasa. These classes give important access to information not typically shared with baristas, cafe managers, or roasters.

Klasik Bean's work has not only helped return hundreds of hectares of unclaimed farmland back to natives, but was also awarded an official farmers cooperative status by the government, and earned Purnomowidi a lifetime sustainability award through the Specialty Coffee Association. Indonesian coffee would not be a thing without Purnomowidi and the team at Klasik Beans.

Another pioneer in the rise of Indonesian specialty coffee is Michail Seno, a cafe lead in Bali, who has taken advantage of the short proximity between farmers and baristas in Indonesia to test processing innovations more efficiently and seamlessly, both on the farm and in the cafe. With near-instantaneous communication possible, he has utilized his outgoing personality to develop friendships throughout the supply chain. This camaraderie and synergy has enabled Seno and farmers to create special coffees for Hungry Bird. He is a great example of how relationships can foster meaningful change in each cup of coffee. Together they represent the countrywide movement of doing things the Indonesian way and achieving results in coffee that wouldn't exist otherwise.

A prime example of this is the mutual collaboration between Hungry Bird Coffee Roaster in Bali with Pantan Musara, a farm in Sumatra. The baristas at Hungry Bird, in particular Seno, have forged a strong bond to Hendra Maulizar, the farmer at Pantan Musara. The communication chain has resulted in a Hungry Bird exclusive coffee— an Abyssinia single-variety processed in the Kenyan fermentation style, which is rarely found outside of Kenya. Relationships like this one have increased the quality of coffee immeasurably in Indonesia in just a few short years, as well as accelerating the overall qualitative experience within Indonesian cafes. New standards emerge daily, and

All Roads Lead to Coffee

WORDS Sabrina Sucato
PHOTOGRAPHS Keng Pereira

It's 6 a.m. and Michail Seno Ardabuana is thinking about coffee.

Not about drinking it, although he'll do just that when he opens Hungry Bird Coffee at 8 a.m. As the rooster crows, however, he's making a mental list of everything the Canggu cafe needs for the day.

A coffee developer and occasional roaster, Ardabuana is a leading member of the tribe at Hungry Bird, the Bali-based roastery known just as much for its fourth wave approach to coffee as it is for its collection of coffee whisperers. By far and large a millennial population, the whisperers, otherwise known as baristas, are attuned to the language of coffee at every level. They know how it grows, how it roasts, and how it drinks. They understand that the art to crafting the perfect latte is nothing without the knowledge of the java resting below the foam or the farmer who cultivated the beans.

"As a coffee producing region, the coffee culture here [in Bali] is growing so fast, and great relationships from customer to barista, barista to roaster, and roaster to farmer, are real," Ardabuana, a repeat award-winner at the Indonesia Barista Championship, notes. "We grow up together, learn together, and help each other."

A former addict, Ardabuana found coffee when he needed it most. He was working as a mechanical engineer for a competitive motorcycle team at the time, and he never guessed a chance trip with his sister to the ABCD School of Coffee in Jakarta would change everything.

"I still remember the aroma, a beautiful jasmine spreading in all the areas at that class," he recalls. "I used to be a junkie, but coffee saved my life."

Like Ardabuana, Kevin Dwisandy is building a career within Bali's coffee culture. As the manager and barista at Alter Ego in Canggu, Dwisandy rises and grinds—literally—to deliver perfect pulls and delicate latte designs daily. Once a cook, he found himself drawn to the intricate flavor profiles of coffee beans, which he says are more nuanced than most food.

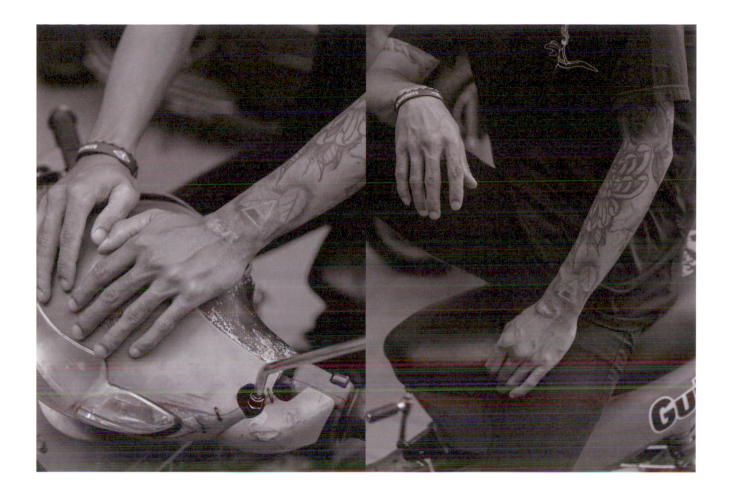

Kevin Dwisandy

Prawira Adhiguna (Edo)

Darrell Jeremy

"To taste the flavor of the coffee itself, you need really intense training or a sharp tongue," he says. "The flavor is so subtle."

Dwisandy is young—26—but he has already worked his way to the heart of the region's coffee industry. It's a good place to be right now, he admits.

"Bali is really open for coffee enthusiasts from all around the world," he observes, adding that he appreciates Alter Ego as a platform to meet and learn from fellow aficionados. He's happy to cultivate his education at the shop for the time being, although he hopes to someday open a storefront of his own.

Dwisandy is not alone in that dream. After all, there's a certain aura of stardom attached to the nation's leading baristas, who are just as famous for their signature latte art as they are for taking home trophies at the Indonesia Brewers Cup and Barista Championship. Individual fame is only part of the allure, however, since each win is shared with the cafe to which each barista returns. At Hungry Bird, where Ardabuana works, for instance, medals collect almost as quickly as espresso pulls, giving visitors added incentive to sample the fresh roasts.

"[Coffee culture] is booming, with more and more local people getting educated about specialty coffee," says Prawira "Edo" Adhiguna, founder and owner of Hungry Bird. Although he spends his days overseeing a team of 20 at the coffee shop and roastery, he can't forget his seven-year journey away from the world of IT and into the epicenter of Bali's java-sphere.

"I love to geek around and the timing was right," he admits. "People around the globe started to take a scientific approach to coffee, which intrigued me."

Now, Adhiguna has his eye on Bali coffee culture's next frontier: coffee farming.

"Bali, and Indonesia in general, have untapped potential when it comes to coffee farming," he observes. After learning best practices from Felipe Sardi, co-owner of the coffee farm La Palma y El Tucan in Colombia, Adhiguna plans to establish a dedicated processing facility and upgrade Hungry Bird's partner farm facility. By keeping the focus local, he hopes to not just educate about specialty coffee within the nation, but also to support the entrepreneurs and baristas behind it.

For at the end of the road, ownership calls. It called to Darrell Jeremy, who took the leap and left his job as a barista in Bandung to open Mannaka Bali, a coffee and matcha shop with a minimalistic aesthetic that allows the smooth potency of its roasts to shine.

"[It has] been a long-time dream of mine," the 25-year-old says of opening the cafe. Although proprietorship drew him to the idea, the opportunity to spotlight local production drives him to work every day. "It became a motivation for Mannaka Bali to keep up with the [international] coffee business market," he admits. Jeremy may be new to the game, but he's confident in his career, one that allows his creativity and curiosity flourish.

And that's exactly why Ardabuana is content to start his days early in the name of coffee. It allows him to channel inspiration into foamy masterpieces, perfect roasting techniques to showcase native beans, and connect with a micro-population that values java, not just as a drink to be savored, but as a universal language too.

"You're not only serving a beverage," he says, "but a joy; joy in a cup."

—

Brutal Beauty

WORDS Imogen Lepere
PHOTOGRAPHS Adam Goldberg, Daniela Velasco

Bali, the mystical island of the gods, has long attracted bohemian Westerners seeking adventure. The crystalline waves of its milk-white beaches and mysterious swathes of jungle drew the surfers of the 70s, who were followed by the Eat Pray Lovers of the noughties seeking an awakening in the many incense-filled shrines scattered around the foothills of Gunung Agung, the island's tallest volcano and spiritual heart. More recently, a new wave of digital freelancers has washed up, launching tech companies and sustainable fashion labels over cold brew and smoothie bowls.

The cafe scene has evolved to reflect this shift with a spate of expat-owned openings that champions a brutalism-inspired aesthetic firmly rooted in the island's tropical landscapes. Dreamcatchers, tribal kitsch, and acid-bright fabrics are out. Neither Western nor Asian, today's architecture nods to classic contemporary names such as Richard Neutra, Marcel Breuer, and Rudolph Schindler. Think clean lines and structures with as little "building" as possible, drawing the outside in through glassless windows and verdant jungles of house plants. Mannaka Bali, a pristine coffee and matcha bar in an open-front space scarcely bigger than a garage, is a prime example.

Another excellent example is The Slow Kitchen and Bar in Canggu's happening Batu Bolong district. This airy, vegetable-focused cafe, with its polished concrete floors and Nakashima-style tables, is located in a fabulously-hip boutique hotel of the same name. Its owner George Carrow, a survivor of the fashion industry who still sells his streetwear in a boutique in the lobby, worked closely with the architecture firm Rafael Miranti Architects and Rieky J. Sanur of GFAB Architects to achieve his vision.

"We used a multitude of natural textures to warm the space. The bar and floor have been crafted from poured concrete with local river stones as aggregate. Bar tiles were made on site using three different types of local sand, before being cast and dried on the roof, while the bar

Atika Nanda, Mannaka Bali

Mannaka Bali

tops and furniture are local teak," says Carrow. This desire to root the building in the island even extends to the sofas. Inspired by American designer Stephen Kenn, they were created using repurposed Indonesian military tents.

The name Expat Roasters is enough to make any Balinese food connoisseur misty-eyed with joy—they are the standard bearer of the island's coffee community. The brainchild of award-winning Australian barista Shae Macnamara, this progressive roastery works closely with small local farmers and has trained many of the island's most successful baristas on its custom-designed La Marzocco PB, which has individual boilers and scales in the drip tray. Macnamara's latest offering, Full Circle, was designed by X+O, an architecture agency based in Australia. It's a double-height, concrete and glass space in Ubud. A marble brew bar stands in pride of place, its fluted sides formed by pressing bamboo into concrete.

"This interactive hub, where customers can learn about different brewing processes, was inspired by the Balinese tradition of passing ancestral teachings down throughout the generations," explains brand manager, Kay Tadjoedin.

White bleacher seating echoes the rippling steps of the rice paddies that can be seen through the windows, while a statement mural depicting macaques is a striking homage to the nearby Sacred Monkey Forest.

At Crate Cafe, a sprawling warehouse-concept in Canggu, the interiors are characterised by contrast. "We soften raw metal beams with natural touches such as upcycled wooden furniture and mint-green fabrics that reference the surrounding rice fields," its founder Maree Suteja explains. "The island's design scene is constantly evolving but is always inspired by nature with an emphasis on homegrown materials." Suteja continues. "It's all about creating a sense of flow and not infringing too much on the surroundings." This idea can also be seen at Canvas Cafe, a project by architecture and interior design company Studio Tropis. The roof installation is built around an expansive almond tree on the beach, which doubles as both a point of interest and natural sun umbrella.

At Lazy Cats in Ubud, the tropical industrial trend is skillfully combined with nostalgic touches that nod to the island's tradition of boho-chic. When German architect and cafe co-founder Alexis Dornier found the site, it was a rain-lashed ruin that had stood empty for more than two years. He set about transforming it into a romantic, ramshackle space filled with vintage furniture in light-rose, yellow, and pastel shades of green that pop against the concrete floor and walls. The *pièce de résistance* is the roof, which had partially collapsed and has now been patched up with glass to create a characterful skylight.

Dornier sees this as symbolic of life on the island in general. "Bali's rich culture is characterised by perfect chaos. Things might not always be as you wish and expect them, but if you stay open-minded and creative, stuff does eventually start flowing of its own accord."

A little like a perfectly-brewed cup of coffee perhaps.
—

For a Time and a Place

WORDS Dale Arden Chong
PHOTOGRAPHS Tino Renato

Wake up, brew coffee, get dressed, repeat.

In the dazed stupor that often comes with waking up each morning, it's easy to fall into the rhythms and monotony of the early hour. And yet, for moments that feel like such mundane parts of the day, they can also be the most important. For many—whether it's for the added kick from caffeine or the simple joy of a quality roast—these morning routines include a cup of coffee in a specific part of the home. For some, it's that chair in the corner of the living room where the sunlight hits just so, while others may prefer the empty space next to the counter in the kitchen. It might sound like an exaggeration to describe this morning ritual as a religious experience, but for some Balinese, it actually is.

Like many cities around the world, Bali has evolved with its ever-changing culture and the people within it. However, with roots deeply set in the Hindu faith, there are still parts of Bali's age-old history that continue to remain in the everyday lives of its people. One of these traditions lies in architecture—literally and figuratively—where homes and compounds are built based on ancient concepts from Hindu texts.

According to Gede Bagiarta, who works on the administrative staff of a coffee distributing company in Bali, this specific type of architecture follows a Hindu set of rules known as Asta Kosala Kosali, which is used for building family homes. Bagiarta shared that this concept is similar to Chinese *feng shui* in that it focuses on the layout and space within a multi-structure compound. "In general, these rules were meant to make the home, which is symbolic for the universe and the people who live in it, to have a balanced life—a concept of Tri Hita Karana, the balanced connection between humans and gods, humans and humans, and humans and nature," he shared.

I wayan wanjing, I Komang Aditya.

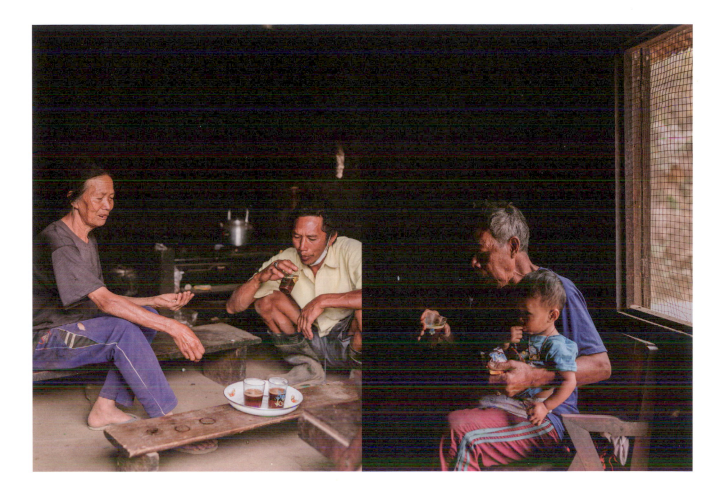

Dating back to the 11th century, Asta Kosala Kosali has adapted over the years and now combines modern technology with the traditional ideas found in Lontar, the Hindu palm-leaf manuscripts. According to an article in the *Bali Tourism Journal* entitled "The art of space and architecture; Asta Kosala Kosali and Asta Bumi," the general layout of homes built on this basis follows the Hindu story of Bhagwan Vishwakarma, the Divine Architect.

According to the rules described in Asta Kosala Kosali, traditional Balinese architectural layout follows the Vastu Purusha Mandala. This is a system of configuring a multi-structure space based on an illustration of a human body drawn in a square grid. This map assigns buildings and rooms specific purposes based on its location on the grid. For example, in the illustration, the giant's head, in the northeast corner, represents the ideal location for the temple in a residential compound. In like manner, other parts of Vastu Purusha correspond with spaces used for other purposes, such as the kitchen or bedrooms.

The center of the compound, photographer and graphic designer Dodik Cahyendra explained, remains empty to welcome deities, creatures, and creation. "Without emptiness, creation cannot happen. In this macrocosmic universe, before creation, there's emptiness," he said. "[After creation] comes the earth,... then the microcosmic creatures. When we build a house we bring this concept of creation into our buildings. The house and temple are macrocosmic and [we, the humans who inhabit them,] are microcosmic." Cahyendra emphasizes the importance this central space carries, mentioning that it's often bigger than each bedroom on the compound.

Of course, due to the amount of space that these traditional compounds take up, most original Balinese housing remains on the outskirts of the city. Instead, families, including Bagiarta's, use the available space in their homes to comply with the practices of Asta Kosala Kosali. "People are still trying to comply with the rules in selected parts of the house, such as the *sanggah*, which is the temple in the house. The rest were built based on available space," he said.

Bagiarta also mentioned that each morning in the *sanggah*, coffee becomes a key component to the family's daily offerings. "After everything has cooked and before we eat breakfast, we must first do offerings to the gods," he explains. "We usually offer everything we cooked that day along with water and coffee—it's a symbol of gratitude to the gods." Once they make this initial offering, they'll make flower offerings, which are known as *canang*.

When it comes to brewing and enjoying coffee for the rest of the day, Cahyendra simply states that there are no rules, as it becomes part of basking in each day. "I will just sit in whichever spot gives me the best feeling in the morning, enjoying golden sunlight with roosters and birds singing," he said. "That said, my favorite one is *bale dangin*, the eastern building. It's always cool and fresh in there." Bagiarta mentioned a similar sentiment, noting that his favorite place to drink coffee is in the kitchen. "It's warm on a cold morning, since the stoves were on duty all morning—and I'm a morning person."

Much like coffee, how and where someone performs a morning ritual can be deeply personal and unique, complete with one's preferences and idiosyncrasies. Yet, with the common background of the Hindu faith— along with the shared practices such as Asta Kosala Kosali—the tasks of the early hour of the day immediately shift from those of a morning routine to something greater than the individual. And while many may see a cup of coffee as a mindless morning necessity, it ultimately becomes a shared experience among those who drink it, quietly bringing a community together—whether they know it or not.

—

Divinities and Demons

WORDS Imogen Lepere
PHOTOGRAPHS Daniela Velasco

It's safe to say that Bali's religion, vivid with colorful stories and imagery, doesn't resemble any other in the world: a giant turtle with the entire island balanced on its back, floating precariously between the depths of the demons and the blazing heavens of the gods; a cracked egg that birthed evil from its yolk and good from its white; an invisible world that's as real as the one we see around us, teeming with spirits who must be appeased twice daily with offerings. This vibrant belief system sees elaborate funeral rituals consume entire villages for days at a time. But where did it come from and how does it continue to influence daily life?

Agama Hindu Dharma, as the local religion is known, has a magpie quality, thanks largely to the fact that the island's population was swept onto its lush shores from across India, China, and Java. It's a fascinating hodgepodge of animism combined with the worship of Buddhist saints and Hindu beliefs that have changed very little for 1,200 years. It has survived two conquests (the Dutch in 1908 and Japanese during WWII) and to this day Bali remains the last bastion of Hinduism in Indonesia, a country that is 87% Muslim.

Ida Bagus Kriyana Putra, who hails from Tulikup Village in the Gianyar region and has been a priest for more than 22 years, explains some of its fundamental principles to us over a cup of Balinese coffee—served treacle-thick and without milk.

"Our core beliefs are to love nature and where you live. To love other humans and strive for success. To pay homage and respect the earth. Caring for Mother Nature is a concept that has been passed down from our ancestors, and serving her is a way of life that also allows us to take better care of ourselves and each other." He goes on to explain, "These concepts are like the personification of the creator. By continuing the ancestors' teachings and passing them on to our children, we are continuing the sacred circle of life."

This touches on a very important aspect of Balinese spirituality: the idea that life is cyclical. Balinese Hindus believe in reincarnation, which is why newborns aren't allowed to touch the ground, which is considered impure, for 105 days. Until this time, they are believed to belong to the spirit world and are therefore not given a name. On the 105th day, newborns' feet touch the floor in an elaborate ceremony at the temple, that sends them into human life of struggle, dying, and being reborn.

This idea is encapsulated in the popular myth of the warrior Bima, the hero of the great Hindu epic The Mahabharata. It's a favourite for re-enactment in *wayang*, a form of puppet theatre performed by artists/spiritual leaders called *dalangs* in mystical shows between midnight and dawn. "We serve coffee as a form of healthy intoxication to the general congregation, from the young to the very old, so it's a uniting drink. And because this tradition has continued for a long time, when we sip coffee in this context, we are united with our ancestors who acted out similar ceremonies before us," says Kriyana Putra.

The story is simple yet profound. Bima seeks his parents in heaven but instead finds them in hell. He offers them the elixir of life but they refuse, accepting the fruits of their karma with good grace. As a reward for unwittingly passing this final test, they end up in heaven. It's a story that illustrates the fact that good and evil, life and death are simply allegories to the Balinese. Unlike in the West where these concepts tend to be binary, in Bali everything continually evolves and mutates, just like shadows themselves.

If Bali is an island of the gods, it's also an island of demons. Locals are heavily invested in a shadow world that has a profound impact on their daily life. The veil between the two worlds is thin: indeed it can be shattered by one beat of a sacred gong. In order to keep the spirit world in balance with ours, and to express gratitude for the blessings of life, the Balinese leave gifts in small, palm-leaf baskets (known as *canang sari*, the simplest form of *banten* or offering) on the floor or near their household shrine every morning. These are highly symbolic. While *canang sari* may include edible gifts, like coffee, cake, or fruit, they will always feature three things: incense, to symbolise Brahma, the creator; holy water that has been purified by a priest, a symbol of Wisnu, the protector; and a flower to symbolise Siwa, the destroyer.

The spirits of dead family members must also be placated. According to Kriyana Putra: "If we go to the cemetery, we bring coffee to the graves of our loved ones as an offering. We'll sit down and drink a cup beside them, just like we used to do when they were alive. It shows our respect for them and is also a way of being together again."

After conducting several decades of research on Balinese culture in the 1940s and 50s, American anthropologist Margaret Mead said: "Arts are part and parcel of daily life on the island, as much as the irrigation system or village community." And this remains true to this day. In fact, the concept of art is so innate to Balinese people that there isn't even a word for it in their language. Villages tend to specialize in a certain form, such as dance, woodcutting, or mask painting and view these activities as a form of communal worship.

Of course, all of this creativity takes time and, in an economy that largely relies on rice and coffee (as well as tourism), you could be forgiven for pointing out that one can't eat a shadow puppet. The answer is *subak abians*, collectives of farmers overseen by those with the dryest plots, who make sure water is shared evenly among the rice and coffee terraces. Even in this, spirituality plays a significant role. The Tri Hita Karana philosophy, which focuses on keeping the balance between humans and gods, humans and each other, and humans and the environment, is the lodestar that governs all of these collectives.

Kriyana Putra concludes: "Coffee is grown everywhere on the island. It makes Mother Earth more fertile and helps to purify the water. Once we mix it with water in our cup, it's symbolic of the continuation of the cycle of earth and water, which, in our religion, symbolises the cycle of life itself."

And what better way to celebrate life than by sharing a cup of vibrant Balinese coffee with someone you love (dead or alive!) on one of the most beautiful islands in the world?

—

The Boroughs of Bali

WORDS David Buehrer
PHOTOGRAPHS Daniela Velasco

Like Indonesia as a whole, Bali has become home to an intertwining weave of cultures, people, and lifestyles. Through massive spikes in tourism over the past three decades, the island has adapted and evolved into a welcoming community of people from all walks of life and locations. The coffee scene here has grown alongside tourism, and has become a dynamic hub for specialty coffee bars, cafes, roasters, and vibrant coffee farms. While the geographical similarities to New York City are exactly none, Bali's swath of cultures and villages has the diversity of New York's boroughs. Full of personality, unique landscapes, and exceptional coffee experiences, four areas of Bali are worth highlighting.

Canggu is located just slightly northwest of the airport in Kuta. It's a quick and sensible first stop after landing, and offers an exciting cafe scene. Canggu's demographic is distinct from other areas of the island. Lots of young expats, who may be overstaying their tourist visas, have found refuge in this westside village of Bali. With Canggu's diverse blend of both Aussies and local Balinese, a thriving surfing scene permeates the cafe culture here. The young crowd tends to veer toward places like Deus Ex Machina's Temple of Enthusiasm, the company's first location outside of Australia. This Aussie transplant features a fully stocked bar, restaurant, cafe, and retail experience. With its strong focus on surfing and motorbikes, the retail side reflects Canggu's unique confluence of cultures, and the sense of freedom that both the island and these sports represent.

By contrast, in Seminyak, you'll find massive hotels, extravagant restaurants, and multi-block luxury malls from some of the world's wealthiest developers. It's not just the most affluent corner of Bali, it's also the most visited part of the island. Almost every Balinese vacation starts in the commercial corners of Seminyak. While some getaways will start and end there, those with wanderlust inevitably work their way into the less-developed parts of Bali. That's not to say Seminyak should

be taken less seriously than other regions. The large wealth deposit here has sprouted some pretty amazing coffee shops with great equipment and thorough fit-outs. Titik Temu Coffee is tucked away on an inner block, near the primary shopping strip of Seminyak. Slightly off the heavily trafficked esplanade nearby, the space must have been more affordable. Instead, resources deem to have been devoted to creating a more modern space. It may have also been one of the first locations in Southeast Asia with La Marzocco's then-newly updated version of the Linea machines. Further down the same esplanade is Expat Roasters, a small espresso bar offsetting the heightened real estate costs by shrinking the cafe to a standing bar. Bright colors, consistent branding, and multilingual staff suggest Expat Roasters and the other Seminyak cafes, like Revolver Espresso, which features a Western-style menu of cereals and sandwiches, are geared toward capturing Indonesians and foreigners alike.

Seminyak may be the most financially vested portion of the Balinese cafe scene, but it doesn't fail to deliver in quality. It's almost inevitable that a trip to the island will take most visitors through Seminyak and embracing the touristy vibes isn't hard to do with so many great coffee options in this fancier part of Bali. Conveniently, Seminyak is also on the way to one of the most unique cultural villages in Bali, Ubud.

Layered into indigo and rice fields, Ubud paints a landscape of the perfect place to settle down. An intersection of many cultures, Ubud is considered the melting pot of Bali. Tucked far away from the beachside resorts, it offers a more traditional Balinese vibe, with winding paths, forests, and Hindu temple homes. While Indonesia is predominantly Muslim, most Balinese adhere to Hindu beliefs. As such, the traditional homes here are more temple than house, surrounded by gardens and usually featuring an open-air pagoda, where meditation and prayers can be performed. In the village center of Ubud is Seniman Coffee. This cafe has a unique vibrancy and magnetic energy that has made it a hub for yogis, spiritual guides, bohemians, and locals. But the cafe is only one of many spaces Seniman occupies on this street. Across the street is its coffee roaster. There's also Seniman Spirits, and a boutique, which sells up-cycled goods, coffee gear, and coffee beans.

Just north of Ubud is Kintamani, the center of Bali's Hindu culture. The largest temples are located here in high elevations. They serve as a gateway to the specialty coffee production of the island. Many Kintamani families have transformed part of their home temples into coffee processing facilities. Constructing raised drying beds and greenhouses out of bamboo, recycled GrainPro plastic, and mosquito nets, these small family producers highlight what's distinctly Balinese about these coffees. Ripe coffee is hand-harvested within walking distance of the farmers' homes. Just as much care and attention have also been put into the practices of pruning, picking, and drying, enabling these local coffee farmers in Bali to produce specialty grade green coffee on par with other origins. While visiting the island's thriving cafe scene, making a point to order these local coffees is a great way to experience something incredibly fresh and truly unique to Bali.

Coffee tourism in Bali has grown tremendously in recent years and, the island's four boroughs of Canggu, Seminyak, Ubud, and Kintamani are at the heart of that movement. Any trip here wouldn't be complete without the context of these cafes and espresso bars along with the people who inhabit them.

—

Where Coffee and Design Compete for Dollars and Likes

WORDS Austin Langlois
PHOTOGRAPHS Daniela Velasco

Bali is one of the 17,000-plus islands that make up the country of Indonesia. Over the past ten-ish years, the island has experienced dramatic change, in part due to Elizabeth Gilbert's memoir "Eat Pray Love" in 2006, followed by a movie version in 2010. Before her book, Bali was a getaway for Australian surfers looking for new waves. It was full of bustling markets with local wares and verdant rice patties. Today, it's a different island. Bali's largest cities to the south are crowded with tourists looking to fill their Instagram with selfies next to Bali's numerous temples and waterfalls. Coach buses packed with foreigners overtake the narrow jungle roads, and gleaming hotels stand where there once were dense forests.

Gilbert's story isn't the first time a memoir has had an impact on tourism. This effect has happened in other places, like Tuscany, Italy (Frances Mayes's "Under The Tuscan Sun") and the Pacific Crest Trail (Cheryl Strayed's "Wild"). But perhaps it's more evident here in Bali because the traditional way of life, with its strong religious influence and modest living, has remained a strong fixture and contrast to the Western influences brought by visitors.

However, it's not just foreigners on holiday who have made an impact on the island, it's also the expats—often interested in the very affordable (some might argue cheap) cost of living that the island offers. Today there's a wide range of foreigners on the island, from yoga instructors to surfer bros, corporate ladder escapees, and award-winning chefs. You'll also find a large number of Australians, opting for the chill island life instead of the bustling Sydney scene. There's even a private school (the Green School) that's popular among expats and their children.

Expats include a growing number of transient, temporary, international residents who travel full time, usually working remotely. These digital nomads have also accelerated change—especially in the coffee industry —on the island. These (typically) younger professionals frequent Bali

Sibling Espresso Bar

for its low-cost living and tropical surroundings. When you're making $1,000 a month teaching English online, you can live quite well in Bali, with rent prices for private villas going for $300-$400 a month (if you're savvy). Those who make higher incomes, like consultants, writers, and coders, are able to live lavishly in Indonesia compared to their home country. With their worldly coffee consumption and strong affinity to Instagram-friendly cafes, they too have shaped what the Balinese coffee market offers. And the locals, in general, seem happy to oblige consumer demand.

It's only been in the last decade, with the influx of expats, digital nomads, yogis, and writers looking for love, that the third wave coffee movement gained traction across the island, perhaps fueled by its proximity to Australia. On almost every street in the trendy neighborhoods of Canggu and Kuta you'll find breezy, open-air, Aussie cafe concepts selling avocado toast and flat whites. It's a dramatic difference from the modest roadside coffee stands serving Bali coffee (an instant powder coffee) and frequented by locals. In fact, locals were quite proud of the fact that there were only two Starbucks on the island until only a few years ago.

These well-traveled and highly engaged digital nomads have brought with them the desire for Instagramable lattes in chic cafes. Instead of an office, they work out of co-working spaces and coffee shops, their midnight conference calls fueled by coffee. They're discerning customers, not only in taste but also in comfort and design. They want a picturesque cafe to share on social media, a chill place to hang with friends, and of course, fast wifi.

While local, more modest, less design-focused coffee shops do exist, like Old Man's Coffee in Ubud (a no-frills, boho-Bali cafe with limited seating), the new norm is exhibited in cafes designed for social media. Places like Expat Roaster in Ubud, or Crumb and Coaster, and Coffee Cartel, both in Kuta, seem to focus on aesthetic as much as they do taste. They often stick out among neighboring businesses that are housed in humble, shed-like buildings. Inside these luxe cafes, expect posh seating, lush decor, artistically plated menu items and latte art. While the quality craft coffee might position them as a destination for coffee lovers, the vibe, decor, and curb appeal likely contribute to a more substantial portion of the business. For a nation and island known for high-quality coffee, the actual beverage is less of an emphasis than the cafe in which it's served.

Perhaps at heart, expats, even with their worldly view, subconsciously desire aesthetics that are familiar to them. Paradoxically, they choose to live in a foreign country, yet still gravitate to spaces and places that feel more like home.

After living in Bali for six months over two years, I can't help but wonder if the impact that expats and tourists have had on the Bali coffee scene isn't happening in other places across the world. It's a struggle that I'm sure many developing communities face when trying to hold onto the traditions of the past while embracing a flood of foreign money and international tastes. It's fundamental to capitalism—the market responds to customer demand.

One can only hope that the chase for Instagram likes and money doesn't dilute the intentionality of the third wave coffee movement or the unique coffee culture of a place.

—

Full Circle: Q&A with Shae Macnamara, Owner of Expat Roasters

INTRODUCTION Thomas Wensma
INTERVIEW & PHOTOGRAPHS Adam Goldberg, Daniela Velasco

Bali is an island of lush jungles and soothing-green rice terraces. This unique part of the Indonesian archipelago weaves international style with local culture.

It's one of the few places in the world where you can drink specialty coffee that was grown and processed a short drive away from the cafe that is serving it. Located a couple of hours away from these coffee farms, Australian Shae Macnamara has been at the forefront of specialty coffee culture in Bali. After several visits, four and a half years ago, he realized the potential for farm-to-cup coffee, but at the standards you'd find in Melbourne and Sydney.

He founded Expat Roasters, bringing an Australian-style cafe experience to the Indonesian island of beauty, style, and local traditions. Opening his first shop in Seminyak, he has been attracting a wide range of visitors. Other cafe locations followed, with Expat Beachwalk in Kuta, and Full Circle in Ubud.

Though met with challenges when first arriving in Bali—from coffee quality and processing methods to business operations—he has been able to make a difference in the Bali specialty coffee scene. Here, Macnamara talks about the flavor characteristics of Indonesian coffee, operating a business and how sustainable practices make current cafe culture in Bali unique.

Full Circle, a concept by Expat Roasters

Where are we right now? What area of Bali?

We're sitting among the jungles of Ubud. Ubud is the spiritual heart of Bali because of the amount of temples, and the focus on ceremonies. So we set up this business, Full Circle, here and wanted to incorporate some of the local themes—whether it's the jungle or the Monkey Forest— in the shop, while staying true to an Australian-style cafe dedicated to specialty coffee and really good breakfast and brunch.

When did you first consider moving to Bali? And what made you stay?

It was about four and a half years ago, I started doing a little bit of consulting in Bali. My wife was writing a book on the food scene of Bali. So we were over here for a week or two at a time.

I realized that there weren't any companies here doing coffee from farm to cup—understanding what was happening on the farms through to the processing, to the roasting, to serving coffee in your own cafe, or training and educating wholesale customers and understanding what's happening with your product at the end. Or, at least, I didn't think there was anyone doing it at the level of Melbourne or Sydney. So I thought, if we come over here, we're blessed to be a couple of hours from specialty coffee farms. Also, it's a beautiful part of the world, with a growing food culture.

Your first shop in Bali was in Seminyak. Why did you pick Seminyak for the first location?

Of all the areas of Bali, Seminyak had the premium dining experiences. And if people are dining out at night in premium places, during the day they would be looking for that sort of experience as well. These days, maybe 60% of our customers in the cafe are domestic tourists. So we get a lot of visitors from Jakarta or Surabaya or the other areas of Indonesia.

At first, we had to attract foreign tourists, so we had an Australian-style espresso bar that we set up in Seminyak. It was very unusual for Indonesians. No one else was really doing specialty coffee at that time, no one had really done an espresso bar that was just coffee. And in doing that, I think our Seminyak location really helped open up a new market.

How did local baristas train before these specialty coffee shops opened?

It was really hard. Before the specialty guys, there were a couple of big international brands that were doing coffee training here. But, obviously, commercial coffee hadn't really evolved much. And so there was a huge desire to learn more, to grow skill levels, to understand what was happening.

In Melbourne or Sydney, baristas are spoiled. There's so much education there. There are so many events. You can go to a cupping session every night if you want. You can learn from world-class baristas. The Bali baristas didn't have that experience.

Also, we've been really lucky because—through my connections around Australia or around the world, through competing or judging, and also having a specialty coffee bar here—we have a lot of [barista] world champions come through Bali. And luckily, they are really open to sharing when they're here.

Proximity between farmer and consumer is unique here, isn't it?

There aren't many places in the world where you have access to specialty coffee farms so close to where you're roasting and serving coffee. For example, within two, three hours of driving, you've got three of my venues that are serving specialty coffee, you've got my roastery that's roasting the specialty coffee, and the farms that are growing the coffee that we're serving.

When you say two or three hours, it's because of the traffic. They're only about 5 miles apart, right?

Yeah.

Also, for the young roasters, to be able to go out to the farms, is unbelievable. When I first started, I used to dream of going to farms and seeing what was happening at origin. I would return from those farm visits and have to do presentations for people who couldn't go. And now we're here at origin, where we're able to ring up producers and say, "We've run out of coffee, can you send some down the hill?" It's a completely different experience.

Are there flavor characteristics associated with Indonesian coffee, and, specifically, Balinese coffee? How does processing affect it?

Indonesian coffee's flavor characteristic has always been associated with Sumatran coffee, which tends to be earthy, spicy, and full-bodied, with low acidity. But when we came to Bali, we looked for regional characteristics and experimental producers that are working with different processing methods to manipulate the flavors of the traditional coffee in those regions. For example, Bali coffee was traditionally a washed processed coffee with general flavor notes of citrus, nuts, black tea, with a medium to low body and high acidity. But now, producers we work with are processing coffee in a variety of ways, including wet-hulled, washed, dry ferment, honey, and natural process, as well as experimenting with different controlled fermentation techniques in Bali. Some of these processes bring out flavor notes such as stone fruit, berries, caramel, molasses, dark chocolate, and even jackfruit.

You've got all these amazing parts of Indonesia that offer different flavor characteristics. But you've also got a variety of processing methods, which plays a big part. So, increasingly, there's not just one traditional outcome. Back in the day, right, you might say, "Brazil's [coffee] tastes like this. Indonesian [coffee] tastes like this. Ethiopian tastes like that." But now, you drink coffee in Indonesia, where we've worked with the processing, or we've worked on the farming—altitude versus other varietals versus the whatever—and you may get a coffee that tastes similar to a Costa Rican [coffee], or what you consider Costa Rican.

Do you export your coffee outside of Indonesia? Or is it mostly for local consumption?

I didn't come over here to do export. I came over here to work with Indonesian coffee culture and see what we can do in Indonesia. Export is challenging. I can't taste the coffee when it arrives. Unless I know it's really good and the customer is happy to pay the extra cost to get it there—you know, it's my brand. I don't have too many things in life, but my brand is one of those things I want to protect. We air freight to a few places, places we know have got great machinery, well-trained baristas. I fly my trainer over to Singapore, for instance, for training sessions. But it becomes expensive.

Tell us a little bit more about what it's like operating a business in Bali or in Indonesia? What are some of the challenges?

It's ridiculously rewarding but ridiculously challenging at the same time. The things that made me fall in love with Bali are also the things that drive me crazy about Bali. When I came over here as a tourist, I would sit back and watch. I would think to myself, "They're always in ceremony. This is so beautiful. I can't believe they give thanks all the time." I'm a deep believer in gratitude and giving thanks. But now, years later, I'm running late to meetings because there's a ceremony going on and I'm stuck in traffic. And I have to rearrange staff schedules because they have ceremonies to attend.

I'm trying to run a business. But you respect the culture and you love what they do. But running the business and doing that is hard. And

also, you can't open a business without big ceremonies. You're ready to open on the 20th, and the priest says, "Eh, the moon will be right on the seventh." And he insists on doing what the gods want. In the grand scheme of things, you look back and are glad you waited three weeks to do the ceremony. Because the staff was happier. Everybody's happier. And that's more important.

We noticed, when we came into the shop this morning, there was a small offering with a little bit of coffee.
Those offerings are a sign of giving thanks. Whether it's to spirits or the gods, or whether it's for customers or whomever. For the offerings, they put lots of different things in there: food, flowers—all sorts of things. But at most of our businesses, we put coffee in there, which is quite common in Bali. Our guys are quite funny about making sure that they get a nice single-origin, properly extracted coffee. It's not leftover coffee from the day before.

What's unique about the cafe culture of Bali now?
I think Bali is a leader in sustainable practices. There's a lot of rubbish on our beaches and on the street. But the culture here recently shifted, and we really hit the ground running, restricting plastics, especially single-use plastics. There are a lot of up-cycling and food waste management programs now. But everyone's doing it themselves—there's no government-driven program. So the people are driving it, which is good. In cafes, there's recycling, up-cycling, and biodegradables.

Also, in Bali, there's a huge push on milk alternatives. In any regional cafe, you'll find at least three different options. And a lot of them are made in-store. We make our milk [alternatives] here at the shop. And I think there's consciousness about how that benefits the environment. There's a lot of these kinds of things happening in Bali that aren't happening with such great detail anywhere else.

You started with Seminyak, then opened Beachwalk, and then Full Circle in Ubud? Do you have plans of opening more?
Our core business is wholesale. And I'm trying to remind myself of that a lot lately. I get really passionate about opening cafes. And I love doing it and I love the interaction with customers. But wholesale's amazing too. By training baristas and creating communities, we get access to a lot of people. We might supply coffee to 200 to 300 venues around Indonesia. If every venue has three or four baristas, we've got a community of 1,000 coffee guys and girls. Each of our cafes has about three, so that's about 20 baristas that work for me. But with wholesale, I've got access to 1,000. The difference we can make in the specialty coffee scene here through wholesale is amazing. But as far as opening more cafes go—who knows?

—

Jamu

WORDS Santiago Rodriguez Tarditi
IllUSTRATION Ole Tillmann (MouseMouse)

As kombucha spigots promise probiotics galore, cold-press juices offer an alternative to flu shots, and bespoke elixirs are concocted to align specific chakras, where does *jamu* stand? The golden beverage—ubiquitous across Bali's wellness boutiques and yoga studios, where it competes with lattes—technically falls under the tonic category. And surprisingly, in this land where coffee abounds, herbal drinks like *jamu* command an outsized market share.

The unspoiled volcanic enclave of Bali is a meeting ground for the digital nomads lining their computers on the counters of Canggu's coffee shops, as well as the spiritual travelers seeking respite in Ubud's *shalas*, and the sunkissed surfers at Uluwatu, all of who seek maximum well-being for optimal performance. Upon arriving, visitors will realize that organic, local, and in most cases vegetarian and vegan foods dominate most menus, with teas and herbal drinks crowding out sodas and booze. Amongst this offering, *jamu* draws attention not just for its shimmering hue, but also for its curative properties.

Although there are a variety of recipes for *jamu*, the drink is usually the result of mixing turmeric, ginger, lime, and a sweetener (customarily honey or agave). Other more elaborate recipes call for tamarind, *kencur* (a kind of ginger also known as resurrection lily) or, in more contemporary preparations, adaptogen additions such as *ashwagandha* and *cordyceps*, two kinds of mushrooms that have healing properties and are reputed to boost brain function. In Ayurveda—the system of medicine stemming from Hinduism, the central spiritual system in Bali—turmeric is known as Kanchani, the Golden Goddess, and is an integral part of the local diet. Packed with anti-inflammatory and anti-bacterial properties, the flowering plant (from the ginger family) has been used for centuries to prevent, treat, and cure all sorts of illnesses, from coughs to cancer.

The first *jamu* was believed to be brewed centuries ago at the request of ailing royals—the rulers of the Kingdom of Mataram, the last Javanese empire before the Dutch conquered the territory. This Hindu-Buddhist realm was very concerned with maintaining the highest body-mind-spirit standards, drawing on nature for all of the necessary ingredients to achieve full balance. Another theory states that the word—a neologism resulting from the words *djampi* (magical, or holy mix) and *oesodo* (well-being)—might have been first pronounced as early as the 5th century.

Jamu is making a full comeback, with over a thousand companies registered in Indonesia dedicated to selling the mix as supplements, cosmetics, or drinks; the latter of which caught our interest when touring the island. Two brands, in particular, stood out from the rest.

The first is Jamu With You, which comes in a slick, modern bottle, packing quite the flavor. Its concentrated liquid feels part-elixir, part-medicine while being an excellent option to quench dry mouths. Made entirely with natural ingredients including honey and black pepper, the bright-orange drink is usually flanked by its liquid brethren, all part of the company's portfolio: the neon-blue "Ubud Tonic" (made with butterfly pea flower, cinnamon, and star anise), the trippy "Bali Tonic" (made with pink guava, lime, and turmeric), and the fiery "Canggu Tonic" (made with fresh ginger, rosella flower, and dragonfruit)—each with its own healing properties.

The other brand we picked up as we swerved up and down the Javanese winding roads, fringed by a thick tropical jungle where birds squawked and monkeys howled, was Jamu Sehati, a "herbal drink purveyor" that looks less trendy and more artisanal than Jamu With You. Each of the bottles has the production and expiration date handwritten on it, as well as different contact details to reach out to the producers, giving it a homey, approachable feel. The company offers a large, one-liter bottle, promising detoxing and weight loss benefits.

Although neither of the brands contains caffeine, the aureate liquid is so wholesome that a single sip of it jolts your whole body, leaving a sweet-and-sour trace on the tongue and the back of the throat, and a mineral, nurturing feeling in your stomach. It might have been a mix of long yoga sessions, the mystique of stone temples with gods aplenty, or the reverberation of the bath gongs, but we'd like to think that after a few weeks of drinking *jamu* in Bali, it was the potion that had us glowing like gold.

—

APPENDIX

Bali:

5758 Coffee Lab
Raya Barat Jalan Pondok Hijau Indah
No.Komplek, Gegerkalong, Sukasari,
Bandung City, West Java, Indonesia

Alchemy
Jl. Penestanan No.75, Sayan,
Kecamatan Ubud, Kabupaten Gianyar,
Bali 80571, Indonesia

Alter Ego
Jl. Batu Mejan, Canggu,
Kec. Kuta Utara, Kabupaten Badung,
Bali, Indonesia

Canvas Cafe
Jl. Hang Tuah No.45, Sanur Kaja,
Kec. Denpasar Sel., Kota Denpasar,
Bali 80227, Indonesia

Coffee Cartel
Jl. Lb. Sari No.8, Kerobokan Kelod,
Kec. Kuta Utara, Kabupaten Badung,
Bali 80361, Indonesia

Corner House
Jl. Kayu Aya No. 10 A, Kerobokan,
Seminyak, Kec. Kuta Utara, Kabupaten
Badung, Bali 80361, Indonesia

Crate Cafe
Jl. Canggu Padang Linjong, Canggu, Kec.
Kuta Utara, Kabupaten Badung, Bali
80351, Indonesia

Crumb and Coaster
Jl. Benesari No.2, Kuta,
Kabupaten Badung,
Bali 80361, Indonesia

Deus Ex Machina, Temple of Enthusiasm
Jl. Pantai Batu Mejan No.8, Canggu,
Kec. Kuta Utara, Kabupaten Badung,
Bali 80361, Indonesia

Expat Roasters
Petitenget St No.1A, Kerobokan Kelod,
North Kuta, Badung Regency,
Bali 80361, Indonesia

Expat Roasters Beachwalk
Beachwalk Shopping Center, Jl. Pantai
Kuta No.1, Kuta, Kabupaten Badung,
Bali 80361, Indonesia

F.R.E.A.K Coffee
Jl. Hanoman No.19, Ubud,
Kecamatan Ubud, Kabupaten Gianyar,
Bali 80571, Indonesia

Full Circle, a Concept by Expat Roasters
Jl. Jatayu, Ubud,
Kecamatan Ubud, Kabupaten Gianyar,
Bali 80571, Indonesia

Hungry Bird Coffee Roasters
Jl. Raya Semat Jl Perancak No.86,
Tibubeneng, Kec. Kuta Utara, Kabupaten
Badung, Bali 80361, Indonesia

Kedai Kopi Aboe Thalib
Jl. Gajah Mada No.53, Delod Peken,
Kec. Tabanan, Kabupaten Tabanan,
Bali 82113, Indonesia

Kintamani Eco Bike Coffee
Penelokan Main Rd, South Batur,
Kintamani, Bangli Regency, Bali 80652,
Indonesia

Lazy Cats
Jl. Raya Ubud No.11, Ubud,
Kecamatan Ubud, Kabupaten Gianyar,
Bali 80571, Indonesia

Lifescrate Cafe
Jl. Canggu Padang Linjong, Canggu,
Kec. Kuta Utara, Kabupaten Badung,
Bali 80351, Indonesia

Mannaka Bali
Jl. Petitenget No.19C, Kerobokan Kelod,
Kec. Kuta Utara, Kabupaten Badung,
Bali 80361, Indonesia

Old Man's Coffee
Pantai Batu Bolong St No.117X, Canggu,
North Kuta, Badung Regency,
Bali 80351, Indonesia

Ombak Zero Waste Cafe
Jungutbatu, Nusapenida,
Klungkung Regency,
Bali 80771, 1, Indonesia

Parachutte
Jl. Subak Sari 13 No.8-4, Canggu,
Kec. Kuta Utara, Kabupaten Badung,
Bali 80361, Indonesia

Revive Cafe
Jl. Penestanan, Sayan,
Kecamatan Ubud, Kabupaten Gianyar,
Bali 80571, Indonesia

Revolver Espresso
Jl. Kayu Aya No.Gang.51, Seminyak,
Kuta, Kabupaten Badung,
Bali 80361, Indonesia

Room 4 Dessert
Jl. Raya Sanggingan, Kedewatan,
Kecamatan Ubud, Kabupaten Gianyar,
Bali 80561, Indonesia

Seniman Coffee
Jl. Sri Wedari No.5, Banjar Taman Kelod,
Kecamatan Ubud, Kabupaten Gianyar,
Bali 80561, Indonesia

Seniman Spirits
Jl. Sri Wedari No.9-13, Ubud,
Kecamatan Ubud, Kabupaten Gianyar,
Bali 80571, Indonesia

Sibling Espresso Bar
Jl. Kayu Cendana, Kerobokan Kelod,
Kec. Kuta Utara, Kabupaten Badung,
Bali 80361, Indonesia

Suka Espresso
Jl. Labuansait No.10, Pecatu, Kec. Kuta
Sel., Kabupaten Badung, Bali 80361,
Indonesia

The Mango Tree Cafe
Jl. Labuan Sait, Pecatu,
South Kuta, Padang Padang,
Bali 80361, Indonesia

The Slow Kitchen and Bar
Pantai Batu Bolong St No.97, Canggu,
North Kuta, Badung Regency,
Bali 80361, Indonesia

Titik Temu Coffee
Jl. Kayu Cendana No.1, Seminyak,
Kuta, Kabupaten Badung,
Bali 80361, Indonesia

Waroeng Noceng
Jl. Srikandi No.130x, Sambangan,
Kec. Sukasada, Kabupaten Buleleng,
Bali 81119, Indonesia

Warung Ipang Bali
No.88xx, Jalan Dewi Sri, Legian,
Kuta, Badung Regency,
Bali 80361, Indonesia

International Locations:

Boutique Coffee
327 E 4th Ave, San Mateo, CA 94401,
United States

La Palma y El Tucan
Zipacón, Cundinamarca,
Colombia

The Crown:
Royal Coffee Lab & Tasting Room
2523 Broadway, Oakland, CA 94612,
United States

**

*This list represents coffee shops visited,
referenced, or interviewed on background for
the making of Drift, Volume 9: Bali.*

Bali

instagram/@driftmag
twitter/@driftny
facebook/driftny